Susan's Secrets

~

A Victorian Kitchen in Wales

To Helen
Best Wishes
Jenny Kenna.

Susan's precious mixing bowl, still used by Jenny today

Susan's Secrets

❧

A Victorian Kitchen in Wales

Jenny Kenna

ceiniog

First published in 2009 by Ceiniog
7 Teilo Street, Cardiff CF11 9JN

Reprinted 2009
Reprinted 2010

ISBN 978-0-9549828-1-2

Printed and bound at Gomer Press, Llandysul, Ceredigion SA44 4JL
Designed by Jenksdesign@yahoo.co.uk
Drawings by Jackie Cavill

Cover: The kitchen at St. Fagans Castle, courtesy of
St. Fagans: National History Museum

Contents

∾

Menu for a dinner party at the Bryants, November 22, 1900

Catherine Williams, Susan, Frederick, and Catherine Thomas,

Manorbier, 1901

Foreword

I found my grandmother's handwritten notebook, dating back to the end of the nineteenth century, among family papers in a battered old suitcase. The well-worn little book contains more than 70 recipes, and several poems.

Grandmother's name was Susan Elizabeth Webb. She was born in 1877 in Johnston, Pembrokeshire. Her father, George Webb, was a police constable in Johnston, St Ishmaels and Pembroke. The family moved to Little Haven in 1889 when Susan was twelve. The Police House, where they lived, still exists in the village, but is now a private residence.

Soon after Susan left school in 1892 she began working for William Hugh Owen Mansel Bryant, a solicitor, and his wife Lilian, in Pembroke. In 1901 Susan moved with the family to Manorbier and remained with them until she married in 1904.

She began her 'upstairs, downstairs' life as a kitchen maid, but the cook soon realised that Susan had the right qualities to follow in her footsteps, and prepared her for the time when she would take her place. Most of the recipes in her notebook are for cakes and desserts, because during her training this type of cookery would have been her initiation to the more complicated dishes she would prepare later.

When I discovered my grandmother's recipes I immediately began to try them out and to my delight they all worked deliciously well. There seemed something very personal and poignant in making the dishes from these recipes that grandmother prepared all those years ago: it was almost like eating history, the taste of the past.

I think the true pleasure of food lies in enjoying it at meals in the company of family and friends. It all goes back to the real meaning of the word companion: one who breaks bread with another. With that in mind I would like to share these recipes, occasionally giving the flavour of Victorian and Edwardian times, as well as looking back upon Pembrokeshire life.

Some of the verses that Susan copied into her notebook reflected her admiration for the bravery of soldiers. In *The Soldier's Tear*, a sentimental verse written in the 1830s by Thomas Haynes Bayly, the young soldier is leaving his loved ones to go to war. Susan was married to a soldier, and understood the demands of military life.

She also admired Rudyard Kipling's *The Absent-Minded Beggar*. Kipling's purpose in writing the poem was to raise money for soldiers' dependants. Susan also copied, among others, a poem written on the death of Queen Victoria, and the traditional Welsh song *The Bells of Aberdovey*. *The Husband's Commandments* is a light-hearted satire on the Ten Commandments, published in Dundee around 1900.

Jenny Kenna

Introduction

Susan was a quick-witted country girl who enjoyed a happy childhood with a kind, loving and close family. Her policeman father made sure that she was especially well mannered, polite and considerate to others. She was attractive, with long, thick black hair that was always pulled back in a chignon.

There was very little employment available to women and girls of her class, other than domestic service, and many began work, like Susan, when they were no more than fifteen. Large households employed teams of servants, including butlers, footmen, housekeepers, cooks, scullery maids, kitchen maids, parlour maids and ladies' maids. By the early 1900s fewer servants were being employed yet domestic service was still recognised as the largest employer for women and girls.

∾

William Bryant and his family lived in a large Georgian town house in Main Street, Pembroke, which had been in William's family for several generations. The Bryants later moved to Manorbier.

When Susan joined the household there were three domestic staff, including Catherine Williams, the sixty-year-old cook who controlled the kitchen and all household matters with a rod of iron. Susan found this strict and stern Victorian spinster quite fearsome.

The work was extremely hard. Susan started at 6am. The first task was to prepare the kitchen range. This was made of cast iron with two ovens at either side with an enclosed fire in the middle and hot plates on top. Each morning the remains of the previous day's fire had to be raked through and a new one prepared and lit. Pans and kettles were filled with water from the pump outside the kitchen door and placed on the hot plates to heat. The hot water for the family's morning wash was carried upstairs in special containers. Once a week the huge range had to be cleaned with blacking. Servants had many tasks - sewing, shoe-cleaning, washing dishes, laundering and ironing and scrubbing the front step.

Food preparation was done on a large central wooden table that was cleaned after each use and scrupulously scrubbed down at the end of the day. There were few labour-saving devices and cooking was a tiring, physical job. Many of Susan's recipes required ingredients to be mixed for at least half an hour.

Life in service was certainly not easy, and there was little time off. Many women worked far away from their families and suffered severe homesickness. Most of their annual wages went towards their transport home. Luckily for Susan, her family lived fairly near so she was able to see them frequently.

Wages were very low and the average kitchen maid of about twenty earned around £15 a year, equivalent to about £1,400 in today's money. A cook in her mid-twenties earned about £20 a year. Food and clothes were paid for by the employer.

There were few opportunities to meet the opposite sex, not least because of the long working hours. In any case, if there were mixed staff in employment, romantic relationships were frowned upon. Eventually, though, most young women in service found a suitor, through friends or perhaps whilst they were out for a walk. Susan met her future husband in church. In general women in service married in their mid-twenties, leaving their jobs to take care of their husbands, children and homes.

The Bryant family's pleasant house in Morfa Terrace overlooked Manorbier castle and was surrounded by beautiful countryside with the sea just minutes away. It had three spacious reception rooms on the ground floor, four large bedrooms on the first floor, with the large kitchen and servants' rooms in the semi-basement. The house is still there.

Most employers were very strict but, fortunately for Susan, William and Lilian

Bryant were kind-hearted. Lilian, in particular was considerate and thoughtful. When Susan's younger sister Annie was unwell, Mrs Bryant suggested that the sea air in Manorbier would improve her health and invited Annie to stay for her convalescence.

Susan was a hard worker, intelligent, willing and well-liked, and Miss Williams, the formidable cook, gradually warmed to her. It was decided that in between her other duties Susan would learn to cook. Whenever possible Miss Williams would sit her down at the kitchen table and read out recipes for Susan to add to her notebook. It is quite clear from some of the writing that poor Susan had to take them down very quickly. Perhaps Miss Williams was impatient and Susan didn't want to be chastised for being slow. So some punctuation marks are missing and some recipes are incomplete.

Susan became a proficient cook under the watchful eye of Miss Williams. Gradually she was given more responsibilities and though Miss Williams was, officially, the cook, Susan did most of her work.

Life as a cook was very demanding, though the gradual availability of new ingredients and food processes tended to ease the strain. Margarine and factory-produced sausages had already been introduced in 1870 and, ten years before, powdered and evaporated milk was developed. Tinned foods were becoming available and citrus fruits, bananas and spices were more plentiful.

When the Bryant family and their staff moved to Manorbier in 1901, Miss Williams became nurse to the Bryant's young son, Frederick; and Susan, at twenty-four, was appointed the household cook.

Manorbier is a delightful village - it has the sea, the castle and a fascinating history. It began to attract visitors in the nineteenth century and developed into an exclusive seaside retreat. It was discovered in the early twentieth century by the Bloomsbury Group of writers and artists. The railway made Manorbier accessible - and the station was only a mile away from the village. A taxi service was run by horse-drawn vehicles.

Susan was content in that charming corner of Pembrokeshire. She enjoyed the responsibilities of her work and became an excellent cook. Miss Williams was relieved that she no longer had to labour in the kitchen. But she frequently hovered round Susan, unable to resist giving her the odd bit of advice and suggesting new dishes to cook. Susan continued to add recipes to her notebook and she never parted with it. It always reminded her of her young working life.

The domestic experience of a young woman in service provided her with valuable skills and discipline for the running of her own home. A cook like Susan acquired extremely useful culinary talents. In time she passed this knowledge to her own children and grandchildren.

In 1904, after twelve years with the Bryants, Susan packed her bags and went home to Pembroke to prepare for her wedding. She took with her two precious things - her notebook and her mixing bowl.

She had met a young soldier, George Kenna, at the village church in Manorbier. Originally from Angle in Pembrokeshire and now a sergeant with the Royal Field Artillery, he was stationed at nearby Penally. He had just returned from twelve years' service with his regiment in India. Although young he was already a hardened veteran.

Susan and George on their wedding day

viii

On a summer's day in 1904, George took Susan for a long walk to Gumfreston where the little twelfth-century church with a graceful tower is a scene of calm and quiet beauty. From a hollow in the churchyard, three springs bubbling with pure medicinal waters enhance the tranquillity of the magical setting. While Susan was sitting on a gravestone George Kenna asked her to marry him.

They were married on December 20 1904 in Gilgal Baptist Chapel in Pennar, Pembroke Dock, the beginning of their happy life together.

Mrs Bryant and Susan kept in touch, and so Susan heard that Catherine Williams had remained with the Bryant family until her death aged eighty-three in 1914. In 1917 Mrs Bryant wrote to Susan with devastating news that her son Frederick, a 2nd Lieutenant with the 4th Battalion, Welsh Regiment, had been killed in action at Gaza, in Palestine. He was twenty-two.

After Susan's marriage George was posted to England. In 1907 she gave birth to their first child, Mary Jane (Maisie), then, in 1909, their son, Stanley, my father. When George retired from the army as a Sergeant Major the family moved back to Wales and settled in Carmarthenshire.

In 1938 they moved to Farnborough in Hampshire where Stanley had found a job at the Royal Aircraft Establishment as an engineer. George died in 1946.

Susan made many friends in Farnborough. She was a member of the Mothers' Union and a regular churchgoer. Tragically, on a January evening in 1955, when Susan was

Susan, George and Maisie, 1907

seventy-eight, she was run over by a car and badly injured, and died several hours later in Farnham Hospital. She was buried at the cemetery in Farnborough, next to her beloved George.

∞

I remember, as a little girl, sitting in grandmother's kitchen when she was baking. Even after she had retired from her work as a cook with the Bryant family she always had a baking day. The fragrances and the heat from the oven made that kitchen the cosiest place in the whole world. There is absolutely nothing to compare with the sweet scent of a cake baking in the oven. It spreads a feeling of contentment throughout the whole house.

She stirred and blended the ingredients in her large bowl, allowing me to have the occasional stir as well. I waited patiently until all the mixtures had been poured into the cake tins and put into the oven and then, as a treat, I was allowed to scrape and eat every last smear of the raw cake mixture from the mixing bowl. When the cakes were cooked and cooled, I'd be given one to try and it always tasted like a slice of heaven.

The tradition of afternoon tea never altered in Susan's house. After lunch she changed into an afternoon dress. Around four o'clock the tea was made and the teapot neatly covered with a knitted cosy. Thinly-cut bread and butter and cakes were served on china plates. Family and friends nibbled, chatted, sipped their tea and took pleasure in this daily ritual.

Susan and sister Annie, 1897

Many recipes in the notebook are associated with afternoon tea and high tea. High tea goes back much further than afternoon tea. Working classes would have high tea as their main meal around 5 to 6pm, when meat was always included. In certain areas it was known as 'meat tea'. The middle and upper classes ate high tea if they had had an early lunch. An assortment of cold meats, pies, salmon, salads, cakes, pastries, jellies and trifles were all laid out for everybody to help themselves.

It is assumed that in this case high tea was associated with an abundance of food. Another theory, and perhaps the most probable, is the connection with the height of the tables used at these meals. For instance afternoon tea was taken on a lower table as opposed to high tea which was served on a higher table.

Now it's time for my tea break. Everything is ready to make that nice cuppa. The teapot and tea caddy are standing by with the teacups and teaspoon. When the water has boiled I'll put the cosy over the teapot to keep the tea warm. All that preparation and my tea break is nearly over. Never mind, I'll just plunge a teabag into a mug and drink it on the move. Grandmother would have cringed.

❧

All of my grandmother's recipes in this book have been tried and tested many times. My kitchen, like those of my friends who experimented and tested for me, sometimes resembled a laboratory.

Susan, George, Maisie and Stanley, 1909

Great effort went into getting the oven temperatures as exact as possible. When my grandmother was learning her trade there were no regulators on cookers. That's why she described the oven heat as slow, cool, quiet, moderate, and quick. In her day cooks used to establish oven heat by placing a sheet of paper into the oven. If it burnt, the oven was too hot. When it turned light brown it was perfect for pies. When it turned dark brown, it was hot and suitable for pastry. When yellow, it was good for cakes and when the paper was light yellow, it was just right for puddings, biscuits and small pastries.

Fortunately, we don't have to use that method. My written temperatures are as accurate as possible. But, as cookers vary, it might be necessary to make some adjustments.

Weights and volumes are shown in both imperial and metric measures. They have been rounded up or down to the nearest conversion. Remember, though, to use only one system of measurement and don't combine the two. In order to recreate the authenticity of the recipes most of the original ingredients listed in the notebook have been used. Cake tin sizes vary so you may have to adjust.

Grandmother used plain flour and added baking powder, cream of tartar and bicarbonate of soda as rising agents. This was surprising, as self-raising flour had been invented by a Welshman, Henry Jones from Monmouthshire, in 1846. I replaced plain flour with self-raising flour in several of the recipes, and in a few cases rice flour was used.

These days we are not familiar with isinglass, one of the ingredients my grandmother used. It came from the stomach lining of the sturgeon, a fish that was far more common in Europe in the 1900s when it came to spawn in the rivers. Unfortunately, it was over-fished and isinglass is now rare. I replaced it in the recipes with gelatine which comes in packets containing 12g sachets.

German yeast was also mentioned in grandmother's notebook, probably because the method of compressing it into a solidified state for transportation was developed in Germany, and it was easier to obtain than any other kind of yeast. Or perhaps it was the best. For simplicity and convenience I have used Easy Bake Yeast, which is sold in 7g sachets.

Another common Victorian ingredient was lump sugar, crystallized white sugar in a block used as a substitute for castor sugar. Sometimes called loaf sugar, it was introduced by Henry Tate of Tate and Lyle in 1875.

Turkish raisins were used in one of the recipes, suggesting they were superior to other raisins. Also, butter was used in many recipes requiring fat, with no mention of margarine even though it had been available from around 1889. This indicates that only the best ingredients were used in the household where my grandmother worked. The only convenience food mentioned in the notebook were tinned sardines and anchovies.

Suet was one of grandmother's ingredients, but instead of traditional suet that comes from the fat surrounding the kidneys of cattle and sheep, I used vegetable suet made from palm oil, sunflower oil and rice flour. This is as high in fat as beef suet but it happens to be my preference.

Old notebooks and texts, like the one I've drawn on in this book, give valuable insight into ways of life and eating habits. They were the very beginning of the cookery books we're so familiar with today. They were highly regarded and over the years had numerous owners who added their own recipes and amendments.

Through my grandmother's recipes and notes, and using her wonderful old mixing bowl, I've felt myself linked not only with her, but with many other cooks who made such delicious dishes in their Victorian kitchens.

A Victorian Kitchen in Wales

☙

Cakes

Rich Fruit Cake

The weight of 4 eggs in butter & Sugar
& double the Quantity of Flour 1/4 of a
lb of currants 1/4 lb of Sultanas a few
slices on candied peel one teaspoon
full of Carbonate of Soda put
Butter in a basin and beat to
a cream add sugar and yolks
of eggs, then add flour, powder &
Soda next add whites of eggs well
beaten then add currants & Sultanas
& peel bake in a medium oven
for two hours

Rich Fruit Cake

4 large eggs, separated
8oz/225g butter
8oz/225g brown sugar
10oz/275g flour
teaspoon bicarbonate of soda
teaspoon baking powder
4oz/110g currants
4oz/110g sultanas
a few slices of candied peel

Heat oven to 160°/gas mark 2. Line an 8"/20cm cake tin with greaseproof paper. Cream the butter and sugar. Beat the egg yolks and blend into the mixture. Add the flour with bicarbonate of soda, baking powder and continue to mix. Beat egg whites to a stiff froth and fold into the mixture. Stir in the currants, sultanas and peel. Bake for about 2 hours.

Grandmother's weights have been slightly adjusted. This cake turned out perfectly.

Maids of Honour

Sponge cakes — Jam Sherry. icing of castor
sugar & water — a few drops of lemon juice
whipped cream — Make a sponge cake of 2 eggs
their weight in sugar butter & flour — a little
baking powder, When cold cut in two & spread
a layer of Jam between — Put together again
& cut a little of the centre. Pour over the sponge
1 glass Sherry — When soaked well cover with
the icing fill up with whipped cream the centre
Garnish with a little of the cream or
crystallized fruit — Small penny sponge
cakes done in the same way answer
very well for this dish

Maids of Honour

2 large eggs
5oz/150g castor sugar
5oz/150g butter
5oz/150g flour
½ teaspoon baking powder
teaspoon lemon juice
a little finely grated lemon rind

For the filling
2 tablespoons jam

For the icing
2oz/50g icing sugar
3 tablespoons sherry
a few drops lemon juice

For the centre
whipped cream

Heat oven to 170°/gas mark 3. Grease a 7"/18cm cake tin. Sift the sugar in a basin, add the eggs and whisk together till smooth. Sift the flour and add to the mixture. Add the finely grated lemon rind and the juice and continue to mix. Put in the prepared cake tin and bake for 20 to 25 minutes. Insert a knife in middle and if it comes out clean, the cake is cooked. When cold, cut in half and spread a layer of jam in the middle then reassemble the cake. Pour 2 tablespoons of sherry over the cake, mix the icing sugar with the remainder of the sherry, and when the cake is well soaked cover with the icing. Cut a ring out of the centre and fill with the whipped cream and chill.

Although there are other versions of this recipe, this one turned out to be very special indeed. It was tested by Margaret Bond, a great confectionery cook.

Chocolate Chocolate Cake

¼ lb. of Chocolate
¼ " of butter
¼ " of Castor Sugar
2 oz of flour
1 " of ground rice
2 eggs
½ teaspoonfull baking powder
½ jill of milk
few drop of Vanilla essence

Line tin with paper double thickness
Beat butter & sugar together to a cream
Add eggs one by one, dissolve Chocolate in the
milk - add it to butter Sugar & eggs & mix well
together. Mix flour & rice together with baking
powder. add these carefully to the other
ingredients & pour mixture into prepared
tin & bake in moderate oven for 1 ½ hours

6

Chocolate Cake One

4oz/110g dark chocolate
4oz/110g butter
4oz/110g castor sugar
3oz/75g flour
2 eggs
½ teaspoon baking powder
2fl oz/55ml milk
few drops of vanilla essence

Heat oven to 170°/gas mark 3. Line a 6"/15cm cake tin with greaseproof paper. Dissolve the chocolate with the milk over low heat. Beat butter and sugar to a cream and add the eggs one by one and mix well. Add the melted chocolate. Mix the baking powder with the flour and carefully add to the mixture. Continue mixing for about 5 minutes. Bake for 1½ hours.

I've always preferred savoury food but this cake could convert me. I made it for the Welsh rugby star Stephen Jones. He took it to Llanelli's Parc y Scarlets when the team was playing the Cardiff Blues. The Scarlets won and so did the cake because Stephen told me that he shared it with teammates who unanimously declared that it was delicious.

Cheese Cakes

Wash a lemon & grate the rind add to it
the juice of the lemon a Table spoon full of
Butter 2 of sifted sugar & a well beaten
egg. Put in a small saucepan & stir
over gentle heat until it thickens line
small patty tins with Flaky pastry &
bake, then fill up with the lemon c.
& serve hot or cold. / another way

Take an ounce each of Butter & sugar & be
to a cream then add the juice and fresh
rind of half a lemon a crumbled sponge-
finger and a beaten egg. Beat well &
stir in a small saucepan over gentle
heat until thick then pour in the
lined tins & bake with the crust for
about 18 minutes

Cheese Cakes

Juice and grated rind of 1 lemon
1oz/25g butter
1½ oz/40g sifted castor sugar
1 beaten egg
1 sheet of ready-made puff pastry

Heat oven to 190°/gas mark 5. Grease a patty tin and line with the rolled out pastry. Rest in a cool place. Put the lemon juice and the grated rind with the butter, sugar and egg into a small saucepan and stir over gentle heat till mixture thickens. When cooled spoon into the tin and bake for about 15 minutes.

These could be made with shortcrust pastry. For an alternative filling add 1oz/25g of cake crumbs and ¼ teaspoon of powdered ginger to the lemon mixture. It's odd they are called cheese cakes as they are really lemon curd cakes. Whatever the description they are very tasty.

A nice plain cake

1 lb of Flour. ¼ lb of butter ½ lb of sugar ½ lb
of Currants 2 ozs of candied peel ½ pt of milk
one teaspoonful of ~~the~~ carbonate of soda —
Put the flour into a basin with the sugar
currants & sliced candied peel — beat the butter
to a cream and mix all these together with
the milk

Stir the Ammonia or Carbonate of Soda set
into a table spoonful of milk — Add it to the
dough & beat the whole well untill everything
is throughly mixed Put into a buttered
tin & bake from 1½ to 2 hours

Nice Plain Cake

1lb/450g self-raising flour
4oz/110g butter
8oz/225g castor sugar
8oz/225g currants
10fl oz/275ml milk
teaspoon bicarbonate of soda mixed with tablespoon milk
2oz/50g candied peel, optional

Heat oven to 150°/gas mark 2. Line an 8"/20cm cake tin with greaseproof paper. Beat the butter to a cream and add the flour, sugar and fruit. Gradually add the milk and stir in the bicarbonate of soda. Beat well until blended. Bake for 1½ hours.

I was delighted that the confectionery chef at the Stradey Park Hotel in Llanelli tested this cake, and said it was extremely nice, and not really plain at all. She found it worked better with self-raising flour, and added that it did not rise very much, probably due to the fact there were no eggs in the recipe. The hotel was generous, and baked this cake, as well as another two from the notebook, for the Pembrokeshire Historic Buildings Trust to have for tea after the AGM in Little Newcastle, Pembrokeshire. The members loved them.

Meringues

Whites of 2 eggs 2 oz Castor Sugar beat
the whites till stiff then add the Sugar
& beat together till stiff enough to stand
put some greased paper on a tin put
the whites & sugar on this in rows with
a dessert Spoon Bake in a very
cool oven (½ hr) till the meringues
are set on the top turn out over Scoop
out the inside & put in the oven again
till the inside are dry fill with
whiped Cream the Spoon with which
the meringues are formed should be
Silver & must first be dipped in Cold
water Before baking a little Castor
Sugar be sprinkled on the meringues

Meringues

2 large egg whites
4oz/110g castor sugar
whipped cream

Heat oven to 140°/gas mark 1. Have ready an oven tray lined with greaseproof paper. Whisk the egg whites till stiff. Gradually add the sugar and beat until stiff enough to stand. With a dessertspoon put mixture in rows on the baking tray and sprinkle with a little sugar and bake until the meringues are set on top. When this stage is reached bring out of the oven, scoop out the insides and return to the oven for meringues to dry out. This takes about another 30 minutes. When cooked and cooled fill with the whipped cream.

Grandmother mentioned using a silver spoon first dipped in water. But my silver spoon was yellow so I used a stainless steel one instead. This recipe comes with a health warning! If you're frothing the egg whites by hand it's a painful business. They take a great deal of beating before they become stiff, and my arm ached for ages afterwards. An electric hand whisk is better.

Angel Cake

Beat the whites only of 6 eggs to a froth
add 4 oz of castor sugar 1 teaspoonful
Vanilla flavouring. When beaten again
stir in 4½ oz of finely sifted & warm dry
flour; Pour at once in a buttered tin
& bake in a moderate oven   Mrs Withington

The Soldiers Tear

Upon the Hill he turned
To take the last fond look
Of the Valley and the Village church
And the cottage by the Brook
He listened to the sounds
So familiar to his ear
And the Soldier leant upon his Sword
And wiped away a tear

Angel Cake

6 egg whites
6oz/175g sifted castor sugar
4½oz/125g sifted flour
teaspoon vanilla essence

Heat oven to 170°/gas mark 3. Grease a 7"/18cm sandwich tin. Beat the egg whites to a stiff froth. Add the sugar and vanilla essence. When beaten fold in the flour. Pour into the tin immediately. Bake for 30 minutes.

I wondered if I'd followed the recipe correctly because when cooked the cake had a strange bouncy feel. After consulting Mrs Beeton my mind was put at rest because she says: 'When the cake springs back on finger pressure it's considered ready.' So my cake was spot on and tasted good. Diana Lidstone, an experienced cook, also tried the recipe using half the above ingredients. It turned out well, but she found it a little too sweet. So, if you prefer, use less sugar.

Cocoanut fingers

½ lb Des. cocoanut
¼ lb Sugar
¼ lb Butter
2 oz Flour
3 eggs
½ teaspoonfull baking powder

Cream butter & sugar together add one eggs
one at a time - Then add cocoanut & lastly
Flour & baking powder to-gether
Pour mixture into a tin which has been greased
& lined with paper & bake in quick oven
for 10 minutes Turn out onto a piece of
paper sprinkled with Sugar & cocoanut
Ice with glaze icing & Sprinkle with with
cocoanut & cut into fancy shapes

Coconut Fingers

8oz/225g desiccated coconut
8oz/225g castor sugar
4oz/110g butter
2oz/50g flour
3 eggs
½ teaspoon baking powder

Heat oven to 190°/gas mark 5. Line an oven tray with greaseproof paper.
Cream the butter and sugar and add the eggs one at a time. Add coconut and continue to mix well. Blend in the flour and baking powder. Bake for 10 minutes or until golden. When cool cut into fingers.

These were a real success and easy to make, so it was an excellent recipe for a cookery workshop I held at Ysgol y Castell primary school in Kidwelly. The children thoroughly enjoyed hearing about Susan, and making her recipe in the classroom. As the coconut fingers cook quickly the children sat in front of the oven and waited until they were done. Not a single crumb was left.

Sultana Cake

½ lb Flour rub in 4 oz butter with tips of fingers
1 teaspoonfull baking powder 5 oz Castor
Sugar 4 oz Sultanas & the rind of a lemon 1 oz
of Candied peel. Moison with the yolk of 2 eggs
½ gill of milk. Stir all up with wooden spoon
Whisk the whites to stiff froth with a knife
Add to the mixture Bake in a tin for 1½ hours

Beside the at-cottage porch
A girl was on her knees
She held aloft a snowy scarf
Which fluttered in the breeze.
She breathed a prayer for him
A prayer he could not hear
But he paused to bless her as she knelt
And wiped away a tear

Sultana Cake

8oz/225g flour
4oz/110g castor sugar
4oz/110g butter
4oz/110g sultanas
finely grated rind of 1 lemon
1oz/25g candied peel, optional
2 eggs, separated
teaspoon baking powder
4fl oz/110ml milk

Heat oven to 170°/gas mark 3. Line a 6"/15cm cake tin with greaseproof paper. Rub the butter, flour, sugar and baking powder together till it resembles breadcrumbs. Add the sultanas, candied peel and grated lemon rind. Moisten with the egg yolks and the milk. Stir with a wooden spoon till blended. Whisk the egg whites to a stiff froth and fold into the mixture. Bake for 1½ hrs.

I made this cake on the day I was going to see my old chum Victor Spinetti in his one-man show at the Grand Theatre, Swansea. I took him a few slices as a treat. He phoned to tell me that the cake was 'absolutely fantastic'!

Balmoral Tartlets

2 oz Butter   1 egg   1 lb Cake Crumbs

2 oz Castor Sugar 1 oz glacé Cherries ½ oz Corn Flour

2 oz Candied Peel

Cream Butter & Sugar together add yolk of egg
& mix well – Add Cake crumbs corn Flour Cherries
& Candied Peel (the last two finely chopped
Chopped. Beat up whites of eggs to stiff froth
& mix with mixture. Line some patty pans &
half fill with this mixture, Put two strips
of Pastry across the top & bake in quick
oven for ¼ of hour (short Crust)

Balmoral Tartlets

For the shortcrust pastry
2oz/50g flour
1oz/25g butter
pinch of salt
cold water to mix

For the filling
2oz/50g butter
1oz/ 25g cake crumbs
2oz/50g castor sugar
1oz/25g finely chopped glacé cherries
½oz/10g cornflour
1 egg, separated

Heat oven to 180°/gas mark 4. Grease a patty tin. Rub together the butter, flour and salt. Add water little by little till the correct consistency is achieved. Thoroughly knead the pastry and leave to rest in a cool place. Cream the butter and sugar, add the egg yolk and mix well. Blend in the cake crumbs, cornflour and cherries. Beat the egg white to a froth and fold into the mixture. Roll out the pastry and cut into rings to line the patty tin, using a pastry ring or the top of a glass. Reserve a little pastry for the tops of the tarts. Spoon the filling into the pastry cases and put two strips of pastry across the top of each. Bake for 15 to 20 minutes.

These are nice, and surprisingly easy to make.

Sponge Cake

5 eggs   the weight of 4 oz Caster Sugar
              "   "   3 oz Flour
a little grated rind or essence of lemon
Sift the Sugar in a Basin add the
x the eggs whisk both together about
about 20 minutes or until the mixture
begins to thicken then Sift in the
Flour add flavouring pour into a
x greased Mould & Bake in a
moderate oven for 1¼ hours

N B
        Never take a Sponge Cake out
of the oven while baking as it
causes it to fall if the oven gets to
hot Cool it Without removing the Cake

Sponge Cake

5 eggs
8oz/225g castor sugar
6oz/175g flour
teaspoon lemon juice
½ teaspoon grated lemon rind

Heat oven to 180°/gas mark 4. Grease and line a 7"/18cm cake tin. Sift the sugar in a basin. Add the eggs and whisk together for about 20 minutes or until the mixture begins to thicken. Sift the flour and add to the mixture. Add the grated lemon and the lemon juice and mix well. Cook for 1¼ hours.

Grandmother advised never to take a sponge cake out of the oven while it's baking as it causes it to fall. If the oven gets too hot, cool it without removing the cake. Margaret Bond tried out this recipe. She was amazed at how much the sponge had risen, so she photographed it. She now uses this recipe all the time.

Potato Currant Cake

Mix well together one lb of mashed potato. 1 lb of flour 8 g. of dripping 4 g. currants lastly one table spoonful boil sufficient water to make it into a dough cut into small pieces & form into buns Bake 20 minutes to be eaten hot cut them through & spread with Golden Syrup

Potato Currant Cake

1lb/450g mashed potatoes
1lb/450g flour
8oz/225g shredded suet
4oz/110g currants
4oz/110g brown sugar
tablespoon water or more if required

Heat oven to 180°/gas mark 4. Grease several baking trays. Mix all the ingredients together into a dough. Cut into small pieces and form into buns. Bake for 20 minutes. Cut in half and spread with golden syrup or honey and eat hot.

Tricia Stone in New Zealand made this and said it was 'good for feeding empty tummies'.

~~Scotch~~ Scotch Shortbread

½ lb Flour ¼ lb Butter 2 g. fine Sugar.
Fresh butter is best; put the above 3
things down on the cake board & first
of all knead the butter & sugar together
then gradually knead both into the flour
or rather knead the Flour into them
until you have all into a firm lump
Divide this into two make each piece
quite round and about ½ inch thick.
pinch the edges prick the top over with
a fork flour on oven shelf, put it on,
& bake it in a quiet oven till it is a
pale yellow brown

26

Scotch Shortbread

8oz/225g flour
4oz/110g butter
2oz/50g castor sugar

Heat oven to 180°/gas mark 4. Grease a baking tray. Mix the sugar with the flour. Gradually knead the butter into it, being careful not to allow the butter to break up too much. When the dough is formed divide the mixture into two. Roll each piece into a round of about ½"/1cm thick. Pinch the edges and prick the top. Bake for about 30 minutes or until they are pale brown and crisp. Sprinkle with sugar while still hot and cut into triangles.

I've adapted grandmother's method so it is easy to prepare and even simpler to eat. The children at the Ysgol y Castell made this at the cookery workshop. We used fancy pastry cutters and made shortbread 'men'. The children made little holes in the tops for a ribbon so they could hang them on their Christmas trees. But I have a funny feeling that they were eaten even before they left the classroom.

A Rich Pound Cake

Beat half a lb of butter to a cream
& with it mix the whites & yolks of 4 eggs
whites & yolks beaten separately Sift ½ lb of
flour & set it near the fire flour with
a little cinnamon & nutmeg mix this
with ½ lb of castor sugar & a little
baking powder the work the dry
ingredients into eggs & butter finally add
½ glass of cherry Beat all for nearly
½ an hour & bake in a greased cake
tin for nearly & hour

Rich Round Cake

8oz/225g butter

8oz/225g flour

8oz/225g castor sugar

4 eggs

¼ teaspoon cinnamon

¼ teaspoon nutmeg

¼ teaspoon baking powder

½ glass of sherry

Heat oven to 180°/gas mark 4. Line an 8"/20cm cake tin. Beat the butter to a cream and add the egg yolks. Beat whites of eggs to a stiff froth and add to the mixture. Work the dry ingredients into it and finally add the sherry. Beat well together and bake for about 1 hour.

This cake got a great reaction from my friends John Siggins and the fashion designer John Bates. 'Rather greedily we ate the cake at one sitting with the delicious Normandy Pippin Mould you also made. The apple and cinnamon complemented each other wonderfully, and our resolution to cut down on cakes has gone out of the window. Shame on you!'

Grandmother said the mixture should be beaten for 30 minutes, but I cheated and just did 5 minutes. The result was still a winner - a delicious and moist cake. It was quicker to make this cake than buy one which would not have tasted nearly as good.

A Superior Sultana Cake

Beat to a cream a half pound of fresh
Butter add the same Quantity of sugar
with a ½ lb of Flour ½ lb rice flour
½ lb Sultanas & a teaspoonful of baking
powder. When those are mixed
add the eggs one at a time beaten
Separately. add about a teacupful of
milk Beat all together for 5 minutes
& Bake in a moderate oven for one
and a half 2 two hours

Superior Sultana Cake

8oz/225g butter

8oz/225g castor sugar

8oz/225g self-raising flour

8oz/225g rice flour

8oz/225g sultanas

2 medium eggs

½ cup milk

Heat oven to 150°/gas mark 2. Line an 8"/20cm cake tin with baking parchment or greaseproof paper. Cream the butter and add the sugar, mixing well. Add the flours and sultanas. When mixed blend the eggs one at a time. Add the milk and beat for 5 minutes. Bake for 1½ - 2 hrs. Test with a thin knife and if it comes out perfectly clean the cake is cooked.

The Stradey Park Hotel tested this. It was the first time the chef had used rice flour in a cake recipe. She also used self-raising flour as it worked better and she remarked on the beautiful flavour of the cake. Her father tried it and it reminded him of a cake his mother used to make. The Pembrokeshire Historic Buildings Trust sampled this cake at Little Newcastle. Susan Webb's nieces, Peggy and Mollie Thomas, were there and took great pleasure in seeing their aunt's old recipe being enjoyed by fellow members.

Queen Cakes

Three eggs, 4 oz butter 6 oz sugar 2 Table Spoons of milk 6 oz flour, one teaspoonful of essence of lemon a few currants 3/4 teaspoon baking powder. Butter some Queen cake pans & sprinkle a few dry clean currants in bottom of each

Put butter & sugar in a basin & beat to a cream with a wooden spoon then drop in the yolks of the eggs one by one beating thoroughly, Add the baking powder & flavouring beat the whites very firmly and add them last 3/4 gr fill the pans & bake in a moderate oven about a qr of an hour

Queen Cakes

4oz/110g butter
4oz/110g flour
6oz/175g castor sugar
3 eggs
2 tablespoons lemon juice
teaspoon baking powder
a few currants

Heat oven to 170°/gas mark 3. Butter patty tins or insert baking cases into them. Sprinkle a few currants in the bottom of each one. Cream butter and sugar together with a wooden spoon. Drop in the egg yolks one by one, beating thoroughly. Add the flour, baking powder, lemon juice and mix together. Beat the egg whites to a froth and fold into the mixture. Divide it into the tins or cases to ¾ of their depth. Bake for about 30 minutes.

The first time I made these little cakes, I followed the recipe exactly and sad to say it failed. Then I realised grandmother had forgotten to mention the flour! Why didn't I realise? So, once again I made them with the flour and it worked. They are simple, light little cakes, and Diana Lidstone said they were a delight to eat.

Corn Flour Cake

2 oz of Flour 2 oz of Corn Flour 1/4 lb of Caster Sugar
2 oz Butter 1 spoonfull of baking powder 2 eggs,
Beat Butter to a cream add Sugar & mix
well; break the eggs & beat all well together.
Now stir lightly into this mixture the corn
Flour, Flour, & powder & beat well for 5
minutes, grease & line a cake tin with paper
& pour mixture in & put immediately
into a moderate oven. Bake for 3/4 of
of an hour. When done, Stand on sieve
untill cold

Cornflour Cake

4oz/110g cornflour
4oz/110g castor sugar
2oz/50g butter
2 eggs
teaspoon baking powder

Heat oven to 180°/gas mark 4. Line a 7"/18cm sandwich tin with greaseproof paper. Cream the butter, add the sugar and mix well. Beat in the eggs. Stir in the cornflour and baking powder. Beat well for 5 minutes. Bake for 35 minutes.

A pleasant and light-textured cake that was sampled by The Mermaids, a swimming club based in the Three Rivers Hotel & Spa in Ferryside Carmarthenshire. They all enjoyed it, and suggested that it would be ideal for people suffering from coeliac disease, an intolerance of gluten.

Coffee Cake

4 Eggs, their weight in flour +
Butter. weight of two in castor sugar
a teaspoonfull of Baking Powder
whisk Butter + castor sugar to a
cream, add yoke of eggs, and slowly
dredge in flour + Baking powder whisk
white of Eggs to a stiff froth and
stir into mixture

Make a cream, of 2 of butter, 1½ castor
sugar, + about a desert spoon full of strong
made coffee. Cut cake in rounds and
spread the cream between it. then Ice the
top of cake with Coffee Iceing.

Coffee Cake

4 eggs
8oz/225g flour
8oz/225g butter
4oz/110g castor sugar
teaspoon baking powder
dessertspoon very strong coffee

For the icing
2oz/50g butter
1oz/25g icing sugar
dessertspoon very strong coffee

Heat oven to 180°/gas mark 4. Line an 7"/18cm cake tin with greaseproof paper. Cream the butter and sugar and add the egg yolks. Slowly dredge the flour and baking powder into the mixture. Whisk egg whites into peaks and fold into mixture and add the coffee. Pour into the cake tin and bake for 1 hour. Mix the butter and icing sugar to a paste and add the coffee. Spread over cake when cool.

Pam Jones from Ferryside offered to test this recipe and made a splendid cake that she shared with family and friends. They felt there was not enough coffee flavour in the cake. So I specified very strong coffee in the ingredients. Pam stressed that icing sugar rather than castor must be used for the cake icing.

Orange Cake

4 Eggs their weight in castor sugar.
weight of three in flour.
whisk yokes of eggs well with castor
sugar, whisk whites to a stiff froth
and stir into mixture, then slowly
stridge in flour

for cake filling

the juice of 3 oranges + one lemmon
about 12 lumps of sugar rub six
lumps in rind of oranges put
into saucepan and thicken with
a desert spoon full of cornflour
cut cake in rounds and spread
filling between it then Ice with
orange icing

Orange Cake

4 eggs
10oz/275g castor sugar
8oz/225g flour

For the icing
tablespoon orange juice
2oz/50g icing sugar

For the filling
juice of 3 oranges and 1 lemon
2 tablespoons castor sugar
dessertspoon cornflour

Heat oven to 170°/gas mark 3. Line a 7"/18cm cake tin with greaseproof paper. Beat egg yolks with the sugar. Whisk egg whites to a stiff froth and fold into the sugar and egg. Slowly dredge the flour and carefully fold into the mixture. Pour into the tin and bake for 1 hour. Prepare the cake filling by heating the orange and lemon juices in a saucepan. Add the cornflour and slowly blend till it becomes thick. When the cake is cool cut in half and spread the filling in the middle. Assemble the cake again and mix the tablespoon of orange juice with the icing sugar and spread over the top.

This recipe is sketchy in the notebook, and it sounds a lot of work. But Margaret Bond made sense of it. It's worth making because the cake is mouth-watering.

Eclairs

Put a ½ pint of water into a stewpan
with 4 oz of butter & 2 oz of Castor Sugar
bring to a boil then sive into it 5 oz
of Flour Stir well to-gether & then stand
on the Stove to Cook for 10 minutes
occasionally stirring it " When Cooked
remove from the Stove & let the moisture
Cool there then sieve in by degrees Three
whole eggs & 6 or 8 drops of Vanilla & use

He turned & left the Spot
And do not deem him weak
For dauntless was the Soldiers heart
The tears were on his cheeks
Go watch the foremost ranks
In dangers dark career
Be sure the hand most daring there
Has wiped away a tear –

40

 Éclairs

For the choux pastry
10fl oz/275ml water
4oz/110g butter
2oz/50g castor sugar
5oz/150g flour
3 eggs

For the filling
a few drops of vanilla essence
7fl oz/200ml double cream

Heat oven to 200°/gas mark 6. Grease two baking sheets. Put the water into a saucepan with the butter and sugar and bring to the boil. Turn the heat down and mix in the flour stirring with a wooden spoon until the mixture is blended and leaves the side of the saucepan when stirred. Take off the heat and add the beaten eggs one by one and leave mixture to cool. Spoon choux pastry into a piping bag and with a 1"/2.5cm plain nozzle pipe into 4"/10cm lengths onto the baking sheets. Bake until risen and crisp. Don't open the oven door during this time. Reduce heat to 150°/gas mark 2 until éclairs are dry inside. Cooking time is about 30 minutes altogether. When ready place on a cooling rack and slit open. Whip the double cream until stiff, add the vanilla flavouring, and when éclairs are cool fill the cavities and dust with icing sugar.

This recipe worried me. As well as grandmother giving no method, the mere thought of making éclairs seemed like advanced cookery. When I had worked out the method I realised how simple they were to make and how glorious they were to eat. This could easily become my signature dish.

Little Short Cakes

Rub into a pound of Flour 4 oz. of butter
4 oz. of white powdered Sugar 1 egg & a spoonfull or two of thin Cream to make it into
a paste. When mixed put Currant into
one half & Caraways into the rest
Cut these as before & bake on tins

The Bells of Aberdovey

Bells that ring so blithe & free
Ever Charming joyously
Oh tell me if any love loves me
Oh. Ye bells of aberdovey
One. two three they seem to ring
Thy trusting faith her love will bring
Say the Bells of Aberdovey

Little Short Cakes

8oz/225g flour
4oz/110g castor sugar
4oz/110g butter
1 egg
4 tablespoons single cream
tablespoon currants
tablespoon caraway seeds

Heat oven to 180°/gas mark 4. Lightly grease an oven tray. Rub together the flour, sugar and butter. Add the whisked egg and cream to make a paste. Knead until blended and smooth and cut in two. In one half add the currants and knead again till they are mixed. In the other add the caraway seeds. Individually roll each piece to a ½ in/1cm thickness and cut into shapes. Bake for about 15 to 20 minutes.

I sent this recipe to Richard Fox my actor/singer/writer friend in Los Angeles. He said the result was delicious. Richard was in the film Titanic and he thought they were just the sort of biscuits that would have been served on board with morning coffee or afternoon tea.

Sponge Gingerbread

1 lb Flour   ½ lb Butter   1 lb Treacle
1 oz best ground ~~~~ ginger
1¼ oz Carbonate of Soda   4 eggs

Warm the butter in the treacle. Add
the Soda the last thing. Bake in a
flat tin lined with greased paper,
in a slow oven

Shines the sun with brighter ray
Upon the pathway gleaming
Love still reigns within my heart —
With hope full of radiance beaming

Sponge Gingerbread

8oz/225g self-raising flour
4oz/110g butter
8oz/225g golden syrup
2 medium sized eggs
½ oz/10g ground ginger
¼ oz/5g bicarbonate of soda

Line a baking tray with greased paper. Heat oven to 180°/gas mark 4. Melt the butter over gentle heat with the syrup. Add the flour and ginger and stir thoroughly. Add the beaten eggs and, lastly, the bicarbonate of soda. Spread on the baking tray and bake for 30 minutes. When cool cut into slices.

I used half the quantities of grandmother's recipe. It was almost effortless to make and the result was most satisfying. To verify my testing the Stradey Park Hotel also baked it. They were surprised at how well it turned out considering the mixture was so runny and once more they preferred to use self-raising flour. Members of the Pembrokeshire Historic Buildings Trust were treated to this cake and everyone said how delicious it was and asked for the recipe.

Tea Cakes

Ingredients 2 lbs of Flour ½ teaspoon ful of Salt ¼ butter or lard, 1 egg, a piece of German Yeast the size a walnut, warm milk.

Put the Flour (which should be perfectly dry) into a basin mix with it the Salt & rub in the butter or lard, then beat the egg well, stir to it the Yeast & add these to the Flour with as much warm milk as will make the whole into a smooth paste, & knead it well let it rise near the fire, and when well risen, form it into cakes, place them on tins let them rise again for a few minutes before putting them into the oven & bake from a qr to half an hour in a moderate oven they are very nice with a few Curranţ of sugar added but should be put in after the butter is rubbed. They should be buttered & eaten as soon as baked but when stale they are nice toasted

Tea Cakes

1lb/450g flour
2oz/50g butter
1 egg
¼ teaspoon salt
7g sachet easy bake yeast
7fl oz/200ml warmed milk
level tablespoon castor sugar

Grease several flat baking trays. In a warm bowl mix the flour, salt, sugar and stir in the yeast. Rub in the butter. Add the beaten egg and then the warmed milk and mix to form a smooth paste. Knead for 10 minutes on a warm floured board then cover and leave to rise. Preheat the oven to 200°/gas mark 6. When the dough has well risen form into 3oz/75g cakes and place on the baking trays in a warm place and allow them to rise again before putting in the oven for about 20 - 30 minutes.

They should be buttered and eaten as soon as baked. They are also nice toasted if they become stale. I halved the weights that grandmother gave and made about 10 of them. I was expecting them to be like the tea cakes we are familiar with, but there was no similarity. They are better described as very pleasant buns.

Chocolate Cake

Two small cups of sugar half a cup of butter
3 eggs 1 one cup of Milk 4 oz. chocolate 3 cups
of flour one table spoon full of
Vanilla essence one teaspoonful of Soda
2 of cream of Tartar mix the cake first
& when it is Well beaten take the
Chocolate & stir it in carefully this
makes an excellent ~~Choloate~~ Cake

Bells that ring so blithe & free
Ever chiming joyously.
Chime ye bells so sweet and clear
Let me still thy music hear
Ye chase away each care and fear
Merry bells of Aberdovey

Chocolate Cake with Rice Flour

4oz/110g sugar

4oz/110g butter

8oz/225g rice flour

4oz/110g chocolate

3 eggs

4fl oz/110ml milk

2 teaspoons cream of tartar

teaspoon bicarbonate of soda

teaspoon vanilla essence

Heat oven to 180°/gas mark 4. Line an 7"/18cm cake tin with greaseproof paper. Slowly melt the chocolate in the milk over low heat. Cream the butter and sugar. Add the flour, powders and vanilla essence. Slowly add the beaten eggs and mix well. Pour in the melted chocolate mixture and stir for about five minutes. Bake for 1 hour.

The texture of this cake was decidedly different from Chocolate Cake One as I experimented by using rice flour only. It was very light and almost melted the moment it hit the tongue. I made it again and presented it to Gavin Alexander, my hairdresser. His only complaint was that the cake was irresistible and put paid to his diet!

Victoria Buns

2 oz of Castor Sugar 1 egg 1½ oz of ground rice
2 oz Butter 1½ oz of currants a few thin
slices of candied peal. Flour

Whisk the eggs. Stir in the Sugar & beat
these together well, beat the butter to
a cream Stir in the ground rice
currants & peal & as much flour as will
make it of such a consistency that it
may be rolled into 7 or 8 balls
put these onto a buttered tin & bake
from 3 qrs to an hour they should be
put into the oven at once or they
will become heavy the oven should
be Brisk.

Victoria Buns

2oz/50g castor sugar
1½ oz/40g rice flour
2oz/50g plain flour
2oz/50g butter
1½ oz/40g currants
1 egg

Heat oven to 180°/gas mark 4. Grease a 6-part bun tin or line compartments with baking cases. Whisk the egg, stir in the sugar and beat well together. Cream the butter and add the egg and sugar. Blend in the flours. Add the currants and mix till smooth. Spoon the mixture into the tins and bake for 15 to 20 minutes.

I tested this several times as did my friend Christine Maskell. The buns were almost like cakes and they were delicious.

A plane cake

a lb & a ½ of Flour ½ a lb of butter
½ lb Sugar 2 spoonfull of yeast & a few
carraway seeds —

One two three four they seem to ring
Thy Trusting faith her love will bring
Say the bells of aberdovey
Ever true my heart shall be
With pure affection glowing
Peacefully our stream of life
Shall ever-more be flowing
Chime ye bells so sweet and clear
Let me still thy music hear

Plain Cake

6oz/175g flour
2oz/50g butter
2oz/50g castor sugar
1 egg
4fl oz/100ml lukewarm milk
½ sachet easy bake yeast
nutmeg or caraway seeds

Heat the oven to 170°/gas mark 3. Line a 6"/15cm cake tin with greaseproof paper. Cut butter into pieces, rub into the flour till it resembles breadcrumbs and mix in the sugar and spice. Add the egg and sprinkle the yeast on the milk and blend into the mixture. Mix well and allow to stand for 15 minutes before putting into the tin. Bake for 40 minutes.

This recipe was unfinished in the notebook, so I became a detective. I searched in old cookery books for clues and the mystery was solved. This type of cake is actually called a Yeast Cake. There are many variations, some using sultanas or currants. It's well worth making because it tastes terrific.

Little Orange Cakes

Mix 3 eggs with 5 oz of Castor Sugar till thick & smooth. Shake in 6 oz of Sifted flour the grated rind of two oranges & a small teaspoonful of baking powder. Bake in a good oven for 20 minutes in fancy moulds. Mix ½lb of icing sugar with the juice of one orange & when well mixed pour over the cakes while warm

Beside his best and favourite cook
the British Bobby Stands
Regarding with a hungry look
the cold pie in his hand

Little Orange Cakes

3 egg whites
5oz/150g castor sugar
6oz/175g flour
teaspoon baking powder
1 lemon
2 small oranges

For the icing
2oz/50g icing sugar
tablespoon orange juice

Heat oven to 180°/gas mark 4. Prepare about a dozen small baking cases on a baking tray. Mix the egg whites with the sugar till thick and smooth. Add the flour, baking powder and the grated rind of the lemon and oranges. When mixed well, pour into the baking cases and bake for 20 minutes. Gradually mix the orange juice with the icing sugar, only using enough juice to get a coating consistency. Pour over the cooked cakes while still warm.

Tricia Stone in New Zealand tried this. Oranges are plentiful there, and Tricia enjoyed using them in this recipe. She and her husband loved the little cakes.

Victoria Sandwitches

2 oz. of Flour – 2 oz of butter – 2 eggs cream
The butter in a Jam pot – pour into a basin
add the Sugar & flour & 1 teaspoonful of baking
Powder

While sweeting out his portly waist –
he issues his Command
his appetite is large and long
His Nose is like the Tan
He liquors up with frequent Sup
And eats what ere he can
While (in the intervals cooks face

56

Victoria Sandwich

2oz/50g flour
2oz/50g butter
2oz/50g castor sugar
2 eggs
teaspoon baking powder

Heat oven to 180°/gas mark 4. Line a 7"/18cm sandwich tin with greaseproof paper. Cream the butter and sugar, and slowly add the beaten eggs. Add the flour and baking powder. Mix well, pour mixture into the tin and bake for about 20 minutes.

Later I doubled up the ingredients using two sandwich tins. When cool, I spread the top and middle with thickly whipped cream and freshly sliced strawberries. I had an instant, delicious strawberry gateau. The recipe details in the notebook are sketchy - probably because the old cook, Miss Williams, was rushing my grandmother as she wrote down the instructions.

Iced Coffee Cake

Beat the yolks of two eggs with 2 oz of castor sugar: add by degrees two oz of fine flour, in which has been mixed a small teaspoonful of baking powder. Beat the whites of eggs to a stiff froth, and add them to the cake last. Butter three round tins of the same size and divide the mixture evenly between them. Bake in a quick oven for a qr. of an hour when cold spread each cake with icing and lay one on the other cover the whole with icing. | For the Icing

Stir 3 oz Butter with 7 oz Castor Sugar till it becomes like cream add by degrees very strong coffee to taste.

58

Iced Coffee Cake

2 eggs, separated
2oz/50g castor sugar
2oz/50g plain flour
teaspoon baking powder

For the icing
2oz/50g butter or margarine
3oz/75g castor sugar
3fl oz/75ml very strong coffee

Heat oven to180°/gas mark 4. Grease a 7"/18cm sandwich tin. Beat the egg yolks with the sugar. Gradually add the flour and baking powder and mix well. Beat the egg whites to a stiff froth and add to mixture. Pour into the tin and bake for about 15 minutes. For the icing, cream the butter or margarine and the sugar and slowly add the coffee. Ice when cold.

This recipe was prepared in a cookery demonstration in Morocco by an old friend Kay Cluseau, who runs the gourmet cookery group linked to the American International Women's Association in Rabat. Kay made several batches of the cake as the ingredients listed above were not enough for the large group. It was a great success and though it is called Iced Coffee Cake Kay suggested that any topping would work. She iced one with lemon curd that was equally good. So this is a very versatile cake.

Wedding Cake

Ingredients   3 lbs of fine flour 3 lbs fresh butter 6 lbs
Currants 2 lbs Sifted Sugar 2 nutmegs ¼ oz Mace
¼ oz of Cloves 16 eggs 1 lb of sweet almonds ½ lb of
Candied citron ½ lb each of Candied & orange
peel 1 gill of wine 1 gill of Brandy:

Mode & Let the flour be as fine as possible &
well dried & sifted the currants cleaned the
Sugar well sifted grated nutmeg, the spice well pounded
the eggs thoroughly whisked, whites & yolks
separately. the almonds pounded with a little
orange flower water Candied peel cut fine "When
all these ingredients are prepared, mix them in the
following manner Begin working the Butter with
the hand till it becomes of a cream like consistency
Stir in the Sugar & the whites of the eggs Whisked
Mix them with the Butter & Sugar, next well beat
up the yolks for 10 minutes & adding them to
the flour nutmeg Mace & Cloves continue beating
the whole together for ½ hour or longer till wanted
for the oven, then mix in lightly the currants

60

Wedding Cake

10oz/275g sifted flour
6oz/175g butter
5oz/150g brown sugar
12oz/350g mixed fruit - currants, sultanas, raisins
4oz/110g sweet almonds, pounded
tablespoon dark treacle
2 eggs

¼oz/5g mace
¼oz/5g cloves
¼oz/5g nutmeg
2fl oz/55ml sherry
2fl oz/55ml brandy
2oz/50g finely cut candied peel
teaspoon baking powder

Heat oven to 140°gas mark 1. Line a 8"/20cm cake tin with greaseproof paper. Cream the butter, add the sugar and continue creaming together. Add the eggs one at a time and alternate with stirring in the flour, the spices and the baking powder. When sufficiently mixed add the treacle. Stir in the sherry, brandy, candied peel, almonds and fruit and continue beating till smooth. Bake for 5 hours. Insert a knife through the middle of the cake and if the blade is clean and not sticky, the cake is cooked.

Grandmother's recipe was very wordy so I simplified it and reduced the large weights of her original ingredients proportionately. She said to beat for 30 minutes but once again I cheated and did 10 minutes. The cake turned out very well but it seemed a pity that such a splendid wedding cake wasn't being enjoyed by a bride and groom. December was approaching when I made it, so I placed a few snowmen on top and it was perfect for the festive season.

Almond icing

to every lb of finely pounded loaf sugar
allow 1 lb of sweet almonds the whites of 4 eggs
a little rose water.

Blanch the almonds & pound them a few at a
time to a paste adding a little rose water
whisk the whites to stiff froth mix them the
pounded almonds stir in the sugar & Beat
all together. when the cake is baked lay on the
almond icing & put it in the oven to dry
before laying the preparation on the cake
care must be taken that it is nice & smooth
which is easily accomplished by well beating
the mixture

to ice a cake 3 whites 1 lb icing sugar lemon or
Vanilla flavouring. Beat it well & ice

Almond Icing

3oz/75g castor sugar
3oz/75g icing sugar
6oz/175g ground almonds
1 egg

tablespoon lemon juice
teaspoon vanilla essence
4 tablespoons warmed apricot jam
castor sugar for rolling the paste

Sift the sugars and mix with the ground almonds. Add the lemon juice and vanilla essence and enough egg to bind the ingredients into a workable but dry paste. Knead until thoroughly smooth. Brush the apricot jam over the top and sides of the cake. Dredge castor sugar on a board and roll out the marzipan allowing it to be 4"/10cm wider than the width of the cake. Reverse the cake, putting the jam side in the middle of the rolled marzipan and gradually work the paste down the sides of the cake until it's smoothly covered, ensuring a flat or even surface. Turn the cake upright, cover with a clean cloth and allow a few days for the almond paste to dry out before icing. Although grandmother called this Almond Icing, it is really Marzipan.

This was not difficult to make but coating the cake was a bit fiddly and messy. It's very important when rolling the paste to have the 4"/10cm overlap of the cake's diameter. I succeeded in the end but it took a lot of patience.

to ice a cake) 3 whites $\frac{1}{4}$ cup sugar lemon or
Vanilla flavouring. Beat it well & ice

Week in week out from morn till night
Down cookies steps he'll go
You will see him take a rapid flight
If missus is below
And then resume his broken beat
With measured steps and slow
The Sergeant on his daily rounds
Has done his game before
And tips A C a friendly wink
From another friendly door
For as the bobbies rise in rank
They do it more and more

Royal Icing

2 lightly beaten egg whites
1lb/450g icing sugar
teaspoon lemon juice

Sieve the icing sugar so there are no lumps and add little by little to the beaten egg whites. When a smooth consistency is reached add the lemon juice, beat again and ice the cake.

Grandmother made a mistake in the notebook weights – these are correct. You should not put the iced cake into a plastic container because it causes the icing to become moist. Better to store it in a cake tin or a paper cake box.

Mrs Bryant and Frederick, 1897

A Victorian Kitchen
in Wales

❧

Savouries

Savoury Rice & fish

Break a 1/4 lb of any cold fish into pieces
& remove the bone. Have ready 2 oz of
rice which has been well boiled in water &
drained dry. Melt in a stew pan one oz
of dripping put into it the fish & rice
& stir carefully. season with a little
salt if needed add also a pinch of
white pepper a suspicion of cayenne
if liked. Mix well together & add 1/2 oz
of grated cheese When throughly hot put
on a dish, sprinkle another 1/2 oz of cheese
over it & also a few bread crumbs put
a small piece of dripping here & there
on the top & brown the surface in the
oven it is an improvement to pour
a little gravy round the the dish before
serving.

Home Nts

Savoury Rice and Fish

4oz/110g of any boned cold cooked fish
2oz/50g cooked rice
1oz/25g butter
a few breadcrumbs
1oz/25g cheese
cayenne pepper

Preheat the grill. Break up the fish and mix with the rice. Gently heat the butter in a saucepan and add the fish and rice mixture. Season with salt and cayenne pepper and stir carefully. Add half the cheese and when thoroughly hot, transfer to a greased dish. Put a few knobs of butter here and there, sprinkle with breadcrumbs and the remaining cheese then brown under the grill.

This is a handy dish if you have any leftovers as it makes a simple supper or light luncheon for one. Although I made this myself, I persuaded John Rubin, a film producer friend to spare the time to try it as well. 'Serve this delicious dish to the music from the film Jaws,' he said,' to create an atmosphere in the room!' He added: 'In these times of credit crisis, there's no better dish than this one. I loved it and did not find it difficult to prepare. Some top flight restaurants should be considering a fish recipe like this. The finished product would do all of them justice.'

Orange Salad

Six orange 1 dessert spoon full Salad oil 1 dessertspoon
full Brandy. Finely chopped parsley & a pinch of
Castor Sugar — Peel oranges & scrape all pith off Put
layer in bottom of dish (Cut into rounds or quarters)
Sprinkle with Salad oil & brandy & pinch of Castor
Sugar Put another layer of oranges & proceed on the
same way till all used

He goes on Sunday to the Park
And sits among his cooks
In mufti — quoth the gallant Spark
A praising of their looks

Orange Salad

3 oranges
dessertspoon salad oil
dessertspoon brandy
dessertspoon finely chopped parsley
teaspoon chopped chives
pinch of castor sugar
pinch of salt

Peel oranges and scrape away all pith. Cut in rounds or quarter. Mix salad oil, brandy, sugar, parsley and salt. Put the oranges in a shallow dish and sprinkle with the oil mixture.

I thought this was an odd recipe. A cross between a savoury dish and a dessert. But it came into its own after I added the salt. I served it as a relish for cold meats.

Russian Salad

½ pt of mashecorre of vegetables.

some aspic jelly

half a chicken or any game

Tablespoonfull of mayonaise sauce

some stoned olives

Tablespoonfull of chopped parsley

Teaspoon full of capers

Decorate tin with some vegetables cut into
various shapes, & white of egg set there with aspic
jelly & stand tumbler or run tin in centre
Fill up tin with alternate layers of aspic jelly
& the dry ingredients mixed — when quite set
pour some hot water into the tumbler &
remove it from the mould — Fill up place
with chopped parsley & the remains of the
mash of vegetables & one Tablespoonfull of
Mayonise sauce a teaspoonful of capers &
one Tablespoonfull of aspic jelly

Russian Salad

12oz/350g cooked mixed vegetables cut into small cubes

half a cooked chicken or any game - about 1lb/450g - cut into strips

tablespoon mayonnaise

tablespoon chopped parsley

teaspoon capers

chopped white of 1 hard-boiled egg

a few stoned olives

10fl oz/275ml aspic

seasoning

Have ready a 2pt/1.2litre mould. Reserve 2fl oz/55ml aspic jelly to use later. Mix the olives, parsley, chicken and chopped egg white into half of the aspic jelly. Mix half the cubed vegetables with the rest of the aspic jelly. Insert a glass in the centre of the prepared mould. Surround it with the vegetable mixture, and then the meat mixture on top. Chill until set. Mix the mayonnaise, capers and remaining cubed vegetables into the reserved aspic jelly. Carefully remove the glass by pouring hot water into it and fill the cavity with the mayonnaise mixture. Chill again and when ready to eat remove from the mould and serve as a light luncheon, hors d'oeuvre or at high tea.

This recipe seemed easier said than done, so I got Valerie Leveton, my expert cookery friend, to simplify it, and she came up with a very professional presentation that tasted as good as it looked. She suggested that peas could be included in the mixed vegetables for enhancement.

To Make a good welsh rabbit quickly &
Cheaply — Take a nice portion of nice
moist Cheddar Cheese cut it small & place
in enamelled Saucepan Moisten with a
little Milk & less Vinegar Stir over the fire
until it is a soft creamy mass. then serve
quickly on hot butter toast & Brown top if like

And makes appointments two or three
To keep in their good books
Eating and drinking and sleeping
Onward through life he goes
Each morning sees some meals begun
Each evening sees his close

Welsh Rarebit

4oz/110g Cheddar cheese
tablespoon milk
a few drops of vinegar

Grease a small saucepan with oil to avoid sticking. Cut cheese into small pieces and melt over gentle heat with the milk. Add the vinegar and stir till it becomes a soft creamy mass. Serve immediately on hot buttered toast and brown under the grill if desired.

I coaxed my friend, the actor Geoffrey Hutchings, to try this recipe. In between his busy schedule he tried it twice. 'The first time I used too much milk and vinegar and the consistency was very runny,' he said. 'The second time was much better. It tasted OK but lacked the necessary touch of mustard to really enhance the flavour of the cheese. I did think that the mixture might be used to advantage as latticework to decorate the top of cooked cheese scones!' He added: 'Out of interest this is my recipe for de luxe rarebit. Make a fairly thick roux with butter or oil, flour and milk. Add the grated cheese. When it's melted stir in at least half a teaspoon of English mustard and a tablespoon of finely chopped chives. Season and serve.'

Kegeree

Any cold fish teacupful of boiled rice 1 oz. Butter
1 teaspoonful of mustard 2 soft boiled eggs. salt
& cayenne to taste p.

Pick the fish carefully from the bones, mix with
the other ingredients & serve very hot. The Quantities
may be varied according to the amount of fish
Time ¾ ¼ of an hour after the rice is boiled

Nothing attempted, nothing done
Save eating and repose
Thanks thanks, to the my worthy friend
For the lesson thou hast taught
So Saunter easily through life
And not do what we ought
This may we get by copying thee
A lesson cheaply bought

Kedgeree

4oz/110g cooked fish
2 teacups cooked rice
1½oz/40g butter
teaspoon mustard
2 soft boiled eggs
salt and cayenne pepper to taste

Carefully remove bones from the fish. Melt the butter in a saucepan, add the rice and seasonings and gently stir till warmed through. Add the fish and chopped egg whites making sure everything is hot. Serve on warmed plates and garnish with chopped egg yolks on the top.

What could be easier. This is tasty and although associated with breakfast it's perfect for any meal.

Toad in a hole

Place a qr lb of Sausages in a tin & put into the oven Then make a batter of a qr lb of Flour pinch Salt one egg & qr pt of Milk pour over the Sausages & bake till a nice brown. this is a very nice dish for Tea &c

Toad in a Hole

3oz/75g flour
2 eggs
5fl oz/150ml milk or milk and water
pinch of salt and pepper
tablespoon cooking fat or oil
8oz/225g pricked sausages

Make the batter with the flour, milk, eggs and seasoning, whisking very well. Leave to rest for 30 minutes. Heat oven to 220°/gas mark 7. Meanwhile, grill or fry sausages for 10 minutes. Put the oil in a baking tin and when searing hot arrange the sausages in this and quickly and evenly pour over the batter. Cook for 30 minutes or until crisply puffed up and golden brown.

Everyone has their own particular way of making this old favourite but Mary Arthur Williams came up with the very best. Her batter ratios, as above, seem to be the secret. Grandmother said that this is a nice tea dish but she must have meant high tea because it's very filling. It's scrumptious served with onion gravy, some green vegetables and mashed potatoes mixed with a little mustard.

Cheese Cream

Boil half a pt of milk stir into it one ℥
of Butter & 2 ℥ of grated cheese, make a
thickening of a teaspoonful of cornflour &
a tablespoonful of cold water & stir this into
the milk &c. & add a good pinch of salt
Boil for 5 minutes then set aside to slightly
cool add a beaten egg & stir till
perfectly smooth spread on hot-
toast dust with pepper & ser
hot

Cheese Cream

3fl oz/75ml milk
1oz/25g butter
2oz/50g grated strong cheese
¼ teaspoon mustard
tablespoon cornflour, mixed with tablespoon water
pinch of salt

Heat the milk and stir in the butter and grated cheese. Add the dissolved cornflour and salt, stirring constantly until it thickens and leaves the side of the saucepan. Simmer for 5 minutes. Spread on toast and dust with pepper.

I kept trying to get this recipe to work but each time the cooked concoction was too runny. I got it right by using less milk and more cornflour. I omitted the egg, finding it unnecessary because the dish is rich enough on its own. These modifications resulted in a quick and easy toast topper for 4 people.

Rolls

2 every lb of Flour allow 1 oz of butter
1 pint of milk 1 large teaspoonful
of Yeast a little Salt. warm the butter
in the milk add Yeast Salt & mix together
put Flour into the pan Stir in the
ingredients & let the dough rise well
covered in a warm place Knead it.
well. make it into rolls let them rise
for a few minutes. bake in a quick
oven Richer rolls may be made
by adding 1 or 2 eggs. & more butter
& their appearance improved by
Brushing the top over with Yolk of egg
or a little milk 1 lb flour makes 6
rolls time 15 to 20 minutes

Rolls

1lb/450g flour
1oz/25g butter
1 pt/570ml milk
7g sachet easy bake yeast
pinch of salt

Heat oven to 190°/gas mark 5. Grease a baking tray. Mix the yeast with the flour and salt. Gently melt the butter in the milk till warm, add to the dry ingredients and knead well. Cover and set aside in a warm place allowing the dough to rise. Knead mixture again then make into about 8 rolls. Leave them to rise again and brush the tops with egg yolk or milk. Cook for about 15 to 20 minutes. Extra flour can be used if the mixture is too runny.

Adding 1 or 2 eggs and more butter would make richer rolls. Sue Batt from Ferryside tested these and was particularly pleased with the result.

Scrape & bone 4 Sardines
              3 Anchovies
Blanch Some parsley & pass through a Seive
mix these ingredients well together with 1/4 lb
best fresh Butter, Some black pepper
Pound them till the consistency of butter
& pass through a seive. Put in a Mould

Sardines and Anchovies

small tin drained boneless sardines
5 anchovies
4oz/110g butter
black pepper
parsley
teaspoon lemon juice
lemon wedges to garnish

Chop the parsley and mix with the sardines, anchovies, butter and black pepper.
Pound them altogether till the consistency of butter and add the lemon juice.
Put into a mould to chill. Serve with hot buttered toast.

My great friend the pianist and entertainer Bobby Crush prepared this. 'It couldn't
have been easier to make,' he said. 'Just for my own taste buds and to give it a bit of a
kick, I added extra lemon juice to the mixture and it was delicious. Had it for my lunch
on some toast and polished off the whole bowl!'

Mayonise Sauce

2 yolks of eggs. 1 jill of Salad oil 1 tablespoon full
of mixed vinegar. A little made mustard & pepper
Put the yolks of eggs into small basin & cream with
wooden spoon adding the oil by drop very carefully – then add
vinegar. mustard pepper & salt – Will keep several days in
a cool place

Thus were they in the olden times
But bobbies never now
Would think of recognising cooks
But by a distant bow
Or drinking anything but milk
They call him "Robert now

Mayonnaise Sauce

2 egg yolks
4fl oz/110ml vegetable oil
tablespoon vinegar
a little made mustard
salt and pepper

Put yolks into a small basin and beat with a metal whisk. Add the oil drop by drop, beating constantly until thick. Add the vinegar, mustard and seasoning.

I've tried my hand at homemade mayonnaise many times, and this was the first time it didn't curdle. It did take time and a great deal of beating but it was worth it.

Brawn

Take a very fresh pigs head have it chopped
in half & the cheap taken off. Thoroughly
clean it then wash well in salt & water
afterwards put it in luke warm water
for an hour or two, till quite white &
delicate looking. Then take it out wipe it
& put in a boiler with water enough
to cover it & let it simmer till all the
bones come out. Whilst it is simmering
pound 8 or 12 cloves & mix with a heaped
teaspoonful of black pepper & 2 ditto of
fine salt. Next make a colender very
hot & take up the head with a
skimmer picking out all bones cut up
the head in pieces about an inch
re & stir in the seasoning
press in a mould & let remain

Mrs Walkers

Brawn

Take a very fresh pig's head and chop it in half and take out the cheeks. Thoroughly wash with salt water and rinse. Put the head in lukewarm water for an hour or two, till quite white and delicate looking. Remove from the water, wipe, and put into a boiler with enough water to cover. Allow to simmer till all the bones come off then pour contents into a warm colander. Pick out all the bones and cut the meat into small pieces. Pound 8 cloves and mix with a heaped teaspoon of black pepper and one of salt. Add to the meat and put into a mould. Boil the liquid until well reduced - to achieve a jelly when it's cold - and pour over the meat. Leave until set.

I could not bring myself to try this because I was too squeamish to deal with the main ingredient. But help was at hand because Valerie Leveton came to my rescue. She made it following the original recipe. She said: 'I bought a pig's head and the butcher chopped it into 8 pieces and removed the eyes and brain etc., as required by current food laws. In a 2-gallon stockpot I simmered it for about 4 hours. I added the spice whilst simmering, but lost most of it when I skimmed off the scum. Half of the meat was put into one terrine which ended up a bit bland and needed more seasoning. The other half I put into another terrine adding extra spices, including some mixed herbs. It was an improvement but still it needed more. I strained the stock, adding enough to cover each terrine and allowed them to set. The remainder of the stock made a good soup base, with vegetables, as Mrs Beeton recommends.' Valerie served this with cold meat, pickles and salad.

Susan, Stanley and Maisie, 1914

A Victorian Kitchen
in Wales

❧

Drinks & Preserves

Apple Jam

7 lb of apples peeled cored & sliced
1 pint of water
8 lb of Sugar
Juice of 2 lemons
1 wineglass full of whole ginger cut & crushed
as small as possible 1 Teaspoon full of Cloves
also cut very small. Let it to boil Quickly
to or 3 minutes then keep it boiling slowly
& stir well for about an hour & a half
the jam will have boiled down to nearly
half the quantity &

Apple Jam

7lb/3kg cooking apples, peeled and sliced
1 pint/570ml water
8lb/3.5kg castor sugar
juice of 2 lemons
pips from the apples and lemons tied in a muslin bag
wine glass of whole ginger cut and crushed as small as possible
teaspoon cloves cut very small

Put all the ingredients into a very large saucepan, making sure it is only half full with the mixture because when it boils rapidly it could boil over. Slowly bring to the boil stirring constantly. Allow to boil rapidly for about 3 minutes. Turn down the heat and continue to boil slowly, stirring regularly. When the jam has boiled down to nearly half of original quantity, and when the original frothing stops and the boiling becomes loud with larger bubbling bubbles, it should be ready. Take mixture off the heat and test to see if it has reached setting point by spooning a little jam on a cold plate and allowing it to cool. If the surface sets and wrinkles when pushed with your finger, it means it has reached the setting point. If not, continue boiling and test again after a few minutes. When the jam is ready, remove the muslin bag. Immediately put the jam into warmed jars. Place a circle of greaseproof paper on the top of each jar and seal it.

Orange Gin

one Quart of Gin the rind of 2 Lemons
& 2 seville oranges ½ lb Castor Sugar
Put the above into a jar & stir every day
for a month, then strain & bottle

Victoria

The great bell tolls to the night
measured and deep and slow
And hushed and bowed is the mighty crowd
On the darkened earth below
What souls of the many souls
That pass with the passing hour
Waketh the woe as the knell fall's low
From the height height of the Temple Tower

94

Orange Gin

1pt/570ml inexpensive gin
grated rind of 1 lemon
grated rind of 1 orange and its juice
4oz/110g castor sugar

Put all the ingredients into a screw top jar and shake every day for a month.
Strain and then bottle and store in a dark cupboard till required.

Here was my conundrum. Would I remember to shake every day for a month or would it be far simpler to have a gin and tonic? I decided to give it a try, faithfully shaking the jar each day. It was well worth the trouble because a really pleasant liqueur transpired. I halved the quantity in the notebook.

Mince Meat

½ Eb of finely chopped Suet ¾ Eb 4 2 Eb of rasins stoned & chopped ½ Eb of currants 1 Eb of chopped apples ¾ of a Eb of Sugar Spice to taste, Place these ingredients in a Jar & add 2 wineglasses of brandy if the mince meat is kept a long time add a little more brandy from time to time

It is she who foremost stood
Of the great ones greatest head
Leader of Strength and Monarch of Might
In the mighty age that is dead
It is she to whose throne there drew
As the swell of the Ocean draws
To the moon above, a peoples love
And a watchful & worlds applause

Mincemeat

4oz/110g shredded suet

12oz/350g chopped raisins, sultanas, currants

8oz/225g chopped cooking apples

6oz/175 demerara sugar

½ teaspoon nutmeg

½ teaspoon ginger

½ teaspoon cinnamon

2 liqueur glasses brandy

Prepare jars to hold approximately 2lb/900g of the mixture. Combine all the above ingredients in a bowl, add the brandy, and continue to mix till blended. Fill jars with the mincemeat and seal the tops.

As with many of the recipes in the notebook, I'd never made this before and I was worried that something might go wrong. I gave a jar to Margaret Bond, for her opinion and, thankfully, she judged it perfect. So I can safely say it works. If it's to be kept for a long time, use extra brandy.

Sloe Gin

3 quarts Sloes ½ oz bitter Almonds
2 Lbs Sugar Candy. 1 Gal: of Gin
Stand 3 months then bottle.
Note a gallon of Gin should be stood in a two
gallon Jar to allow plenty of room for the Sloes
& for shaking it should be well shaken
as often as possible at least once a day
The Sloes to be well pricked before putting in the
Gin G

Heart and brain of the best
Statesman and warrior and seer
Drew to her side and lived & died
For love of her love & her
Statesman & warrior & seer
Truest, and bravest, and best
Fell in the fray from her side away
And now she too, is at rest—

Sloe Gin

12oz/350g sloes
1pt/570ml inexpensive gin
4oz/110g castor sugar
½oz/10g almonds

Rinse the sloes and prick each one several times with a pin - tedious but necessary. Put all the ingredients into a large screw top jar. Shake it at least once a day for a month. Strain then bottle and leave in a dark place to mature for 3 months.

Grandmother's recipe was for a gallon of gin, which is rather a lot, so I made a quarter of that amount because I only managed to pick 12oz/350g of sloes. When it was finally ready to drink, this rose-coloured gin had the distinctive taste of a 'dry' liqueur and was well worth the wait. I thoroughly recommend it. If I can gather enough sloes next year I might make 2 gallons. Or perhaps I shouldn't!

Fruit Jelly of any kind

Put the fruit into a preserving pan with its own weight of sugar boil untill the & skim it untill it will jelly the pour the whole through a hair sieve but do not press it; take what remains in the sieve & boil it a ¼ of an hour for Jam: & put the juice into another stewpan & boil the same time. This method saves the trouble of pressing & prevents waste

And the great bells tolls to the night
Deep and measured and slow
And hushed and bowed is the mighty crowd
On the darkened earth below
For the Souls of many Souls

Fruit Jelly of any kind

1lb/450g of fruit
8oz/225g sugar

Put the fruit and sugar into a preserving pan and just cover with water. Ripe fruit needs less water. Stew until the fruit is broken down. Simmer for about 15 minutes. Pour through a sieve and reserve the juice. Boil the fruit pulp with half the juice for 10 minutes to make the jam. Simmer the remaining juice for about 10 minutes to make the jelly.

This was nice and easy. I used plums and removed the stones when the fruit was broken down. It made a small bowl of jelly that my husband tried on his porridge next morning.

Susan and George, 1927

A Victorian Kitchen in Wales

❧

Puddings & Desserts

Sponge Treacle Pudding

3 oz suet or dripping   1 egg

3 oz Flour   1 teaspoonful Baking (Powder

2 Tablespoon of Treacle

Steam 1½ hours. Turn out serve with apricot or Treacle

By the passing hour set free
Hath passed with the hour
to the place of power
In the life of years to be

January 22ᵈᵈ 1901

Sponge Treacle Pudding

3oz/75g shredded suet
3oz/75g flour
2 tablespoons treacle
1 egg
 teaspoon baking powder

Grease a 1pt/570ml pudding basin. Combine the suet with the flour and the baking powder. Add the beaten egg, mixing well, spoon in the treacle and blend till smooth. Pour mixture into the basin and cover with foil or a cloth and secure well, leaving enough room for the pudding to swell. Steam for 1½ hours and serve with custard or crème fraiche.

There were no problems at all with this pudding. It was light and satisfying.

Apple Snow

1 lb apples 2 oz sugar rind of 1 lemon
3 whites of eggs ¼ pint of water, Boil the apples
with the water sugar & rind of lemon
then pass them through a wire sieve & when
cold add the whites of eggs to the pulp & beat
all up *untill like snow.* & *decorate* to taste

The absent minded Beggar

When you've shouted "Rule Brittannia —"
When you've sung "God save the Queen —"
When you've finished killing Kruger with your mouth
Will you kindly drop a shilling in my little tambourine
For a gentleman in Kharki ordered South

Apple Snow

1lb/450g apples
2oz/50g castor sugar
1 lemon
3 egg whites
5fl oz/150ml water

Boil the apples with the water, sugar and grated lemon rind. When cooked pass through a sieve and leave to cool. Whip the egg whites very stiffly and fold into the apple purée until it resembles snow.

I whipped the egg whites by hand as grandmother would have done. The result was fluffy and as light as snow. Children would love it.

Ginger cream

Yolks of 2 eggs ½ pint Cream ½ pint of Milk
3 oz preserved ginger 2 dessertspoonfuls of syrup
Sifted Sugar to taste ½ oz isinglass or gelatine Slice
the ginger finely put into a basin with the syrup
the well beaten yolks of eggs & the milk. Mix these
well together & stir over the fire for about 10 Minutes
or untill mixture thickens. Take it off the fire
& add cream & gelatine. Sweeten to taste
whisk till nearly cold. The gelatine should be melted
in a little cold water - Pour into a mould & set aside
to cool. Sufficient to fill 1½ pint mould

Ginger Cream

2 egg yolks
7fl oz/200ml single cream
10fl oz/275ml milk
3oz/75g preserved or crystallised ginger
2 dessertspoons golden syrup
1 sachet gelatine
3 fl oz/75ml water

Have ready a 1½pt/845ml dampened mould. Thinly slice or grind the ginger and mix with the syrup, well beaten egg yolks and milk. Stir over gentle heat till the mixture thickens a little. Take off heat and add the cream. Heat, not boil, the water and sprinkle over the gelatine stirring briskly till dissolved. Add to the ginger mixture and blend together. Pour into the mould till set - about 4 hours.

Another easy recipe that tasted delicious. Swansea actor Raymond Bowers also prepared this. He said it was good enough to eat so he went ahead and ate the whole lot and then scraped the bowl as well. I used chopped crystallised ginger, and made meringues with the spare egg whites.

Pine Apple Cream

is made the same way as the Ginger Cream
using pine instead of the ginger Add the
juice when the mixture is cold
Place small pieces of pine apple at the
bottom of a mould & pour in the cream

He's an absent minded beggar & his weakness is a great
But we & Paul must take him as we find him
He is out on active service, wiping something of a slate
and he's left a lot o little things behind him

Pineapple Cream

4oz/110g tinned pineapple (drained weight)
5fl oz/150ml pineapple juice
5fl oz/150ml milk
5fl oz/150ml single cream
1 egg yolk
dessertspoon golden syrup
1oz/25g sifted castor sugar
1 sachet gelatine

Have ready a 1½pt/850ml dampened mould. Drain the pineapple, reserving the juice, and thinly chop or roughly purée. Beat the egg yolk and add the milk and syrup. Stir over gentle heat till it thickens a little, remove from heat and add the pineapple and cream. Heat the pineapple juice making sure it does not boil and sprinkle over the gelatine. Stir briskly till dissolved and add immediately to the pineapple mixture blending it all together. Pour into the mould till set - about 4 hours.

Tinned pineapple is recommended because the chemicals in fresh pineapple do not allow it to set well. This lovely cream is good on its own but could be served with a fresh fruit salad.

Elsie's Pudding

... ¼ lb of bread a ½ lb of Flour 1 oz + ½
of brown sugar + one or two eggs soak the
bread in cold milk + water untill soft
squeeze very dry + add to the shredded suet
[1 2 3] beat with a fork. Whip the eggs
mix with the sugar + the other ingre-
ants line a pie dish with this mixture
+ put a layer of marmarlade or Jam
so on untill the dish is full have a layer
of the bread on the top Bake one + ½
hours in a moderate oven

Elsie's Pudding

1lb/450g bread
4oz/110g brown sugar
2 eggs
2oz/50g shredded suet
4oz/110g jam or marmalade
A little milk and water for soaking the bread

Heat oven to 180°/gas mark 4. Grease a pie dish. Soak the bread in cold milk and water until soft. Squeeze very dry and add to the shredded suet and beat with a fork. Whip the eggs, mix with the sugar, and blend with the other ingredients. Put into a pie dish with layers of jam or marmalade in between the bread mixture until the dish is full, ending with the bread. Bake for about 1½ hrs.

Grandmother had included flour and not much sugar in the original so it was very heavy and doughy. I adapted it and it tasted better. This pudding represents many that were eaten when the notebook was written. It would have been a very economical dish as it can be made with leftover bread.

Normandy pippin mould

as many pippins as will fill a the mould
used. Take out the core and cut the pippins
in small pieces put them in a basin and
cover with cold water and let them stand
all night next day simmer them in the same
water and add more if the get too thick
when quite in a pulp pass them through a
Cullander. add enough sugar to sweeten them
& the juice of a lemon, dissolve 1 ℥ of
gelatine and add

Normandy Pippin Mould

1lb/450g eating apples, preferably
Cox's Orange Pippin or Egremont Russet
juice of 1 lemon
1 sachet gelatine
2oz/50g castor sugar
5fl oz/150ml water

Core apples and cut into small pieces. Put in a basin and cover with cold water and allow to stand overnight. Next day simmer the apples in the same water. When cold and in a pulp pass them through a colander and add the lemon juice and enough sugar to sweeten. Sprinkle the gelatine in hot, not boiling, water and stir briskly till thoroughly dissolved and stir into the apple mixture. Pour into a dampened mould and cool till set - about 4 hours.

Valerie Leveton tried this and said it was very easy to make. I was the taster. It was superb and though similar to apple purée, the flavour was far superior as it was more intense and had a longer lasting effect on the palate. I've made it since and it's become a favourite.

Custard for Seas

½ pint milk

2 whole eggs & to yolks

Boil milk & pour onto eggs when custard
perfectly cold put-in to Friezer when half
frozen then add cream & what flavouring
you require —

To freeze first receipt when half frozen
to be packed into moulds & there packed in
ice & salt & frozen

Custard For Teas

10fl oz/275ml milk
2 whole eggs and 2 yolks
2oz/50g castor sugar
a few drops of vanilla flavouring
5fl oz/150ml single or double cream

Beat the eggs and extra yolks together. Boil the milk with the sugar and vanilla flavouring. Pour onto the eggs and mix. Put into a plastic container and when cold place in the freezer. Remove when half frozen, put in a basin, and beat well to separate all the ice crystals. Whip the cream into it thoroughly until it becomes smooth, return to the plastic container and freeze.

This recipe was strange. I thought I was making custard, but I discovered I was making ice cream. An old cookery book described Ice Cream Custard as a base for most flavoured ice creams. I went ahead with grandmother's recipe and confusing as it was, I had made my first ever ice cream. What a nice surprise when I tasted it - proper ice cream. Now I know how simple it is to make, I shall be more adventurous in future and add different flavours.

Canary Pudding

take 3 Eggs there weight in Butter
weight of two in flour + Sugar ½ tsp in
tea spoon full Baking Powder and
grated rind of 1 lemon

whisk Butter + sugar to a cream

Duke's son Cook's son son of a hundred Kings
so Fifty thousand horse & foot going to table bay)=
Each of em doing his Countries work) and who's to
look after their things)

Canary Pudding

3 eggs
6oz/175g butter
4oz/110g flour
2oz/50g castor sugar
grated rind of 1 lemon
teaspoon baking powder

Have ready a 1½pt/845ml greased basin. Cream the butter and sugar. Add beaten eggs one by one. Stir in the flour, baking powder and lemon peel and mix till blended. Pour mixture into the basin, making sure you allow enough room for rising. Put a circle of greaseproof paper on the top of the pudding and cover basin with foil or cloth. Steam for 1½ hrs. Serve with a lemon or jam sauce.

Grandmother did not describe the method but I discovered how to make it, thanks to Mrs Beeton. This pudding is ample for 8 helpings, or 4 for those with larger appetites.

Prune Gateau

1 lb of prunes 1½ pts of water 2 oz of ~~lump~~ lump
Sugar ¾ oz of gelatine & rind of one lemon
Stew the prunes till tender dissolve the
gelatine in ¼ pt & put in Sugar in another
¼ pt of water Add the dissolved Sugar &
Gelatine to the prunes-Stir all & pour into
a mould with whipped cream up the the
Middle & the whole decorated with split almond

Pass the hat for your Credit sake, & pay pay for
Here are girls he married secret asking no permission
For he knew he wouldn't get it if he did   due the
There are ~~girls~~ gas & coals & bills & the house rent falling
And its more then rather likely there's a kid
There are girls he walked out casual They'll be Sorry now
he's gone For an absented minded beggar they will find him

Prune Gateau

8oz/225g prunes
2oz/50g castor sugar
juice of half a lemon
15fl oz/425ml water
1 sachet gelatine
whipped cream
toasted split almonds to garnish

Stew the prunes with the sugar in half the water until tender, then mash. Heat the remaining water - do not boil - and sprinkle gelatine over it, stirring briskly till dissolved. Add this and the lemon juice to the prune mixture, and pour into a dampened shallow bowl. Place a wine glass or tumbler in the middle. When set remove glass and fill the cavity with whipped cream and scatter the toasted split almonds on top.

This recipe may sound ordinary, but it tastes wonderful and looks great on the table. It's quickly made, and it sets in a few hours - and prunes are good for us!

Strawberry Cream

Half pkt of isinglass a little Sugar 1 lemon
¾ pt cream ¼ pint of Strawberry syrup
1½ wine glass of cold water

Soak the isinglass in the water: add the rind
& juice of the lemon with the Sugar & stir
over the fire untill dissolved; remove
the lemon peel & pour into a basin adding
the Strawberry syrup, Whisk the cream
& pour the other Ingredients on it; gently
stirring all the time; Colour with cochineal
& pour into a mould.

Raspberry may be substituted for Straw
berry & any suitable Jam. rubbed through
a hair sieve with a little water
will take the place of Syrup

Strawberry Cream

6oz/175g fresh strawberries
1oz/25g icing sugar
castor sugar, according to taste
juice of 1 lemon
5 fl oz/150 ml double cream
1 sachet gelatine
5fl oz/150ml water

Thinly slice the strawberries and add the icing sugar. Mash then pass through a colander. Add lemon juice and the castor sugar. Put mixture into a measuring jug and top up to ¾pt/425ml with double cream. Heat the water, do not boil, sprinkle in the gelatine and stir briskly till completely dissolved. Add to the strawberry mixture, blending well. Pour into a dampened mould and put in the fridge or a cool place till set.

There are many cream recipes in the notebook and it did make me wonder how Susan kept slim. She was cooking for others, though, but they had small waistlines too. They ate small portions - that was the secret!

Soufflet omlet

3 Yolks & 4 Whites of eggs

4 oz Flour

1 oz castor sugar

Few drops of essence of lemon & Vanilla &
tablespoonful of some jam

Cream yolks of eggs & sugar together till
quite thick then add Flour & flavouring
Whisp to whites to stiff froth & mix yolks &
whites together. Turn mixture into fryingpan
which has been dryed & grease with butter
Bake in oven for 10 minutes Turn out onto
Sugared paper & put Table spoon full of
warmer jam in centre

Soufflé Omelette

3 egg yolks
4 egg whites
½oz/10g flour
1oz/25g castor sugar
a few drops lemon or vanilla essence
tablespoon warm jam

Heat oven to 190°/gas mark 5. Grease a 6"/15cm soufflé dish. Cream the egg yolks and sugar. Add the flour and flavouring and mix well. Whip the egg whites to a stiff froth and fold lightly into the mixture. Bake for 15 to 20 minutes or until set and well risen. Turn the soufflé out and put the warmed jam in the centre.

The award winning Pearl Brasserie in Dublin kindly tested this recipe for me. The kitchen team said: 'An extremely nice recipe, very simple to prepare. We all enjoyed the flavours immensely and found the dish very appetizing. The texture was very smooth. It was quite similar to an American pancake that you would have for breakfast. No enhancements necessary. Chef substituted honey for jam which seemed to complement the dish very well.' Patrons Kirsten Batt and her partner, the chef Sebastien Masi, told me the origin of the recipe. It was created in France by Annette Poulard around 1885 at her celebrated restaurant, La Mère Poulard, in Mont St-Michel. It specialises in omelettes and has served many famous guests over the years including Ernest Hemingway, Leon Trotsky, Margaret Thatcher and Yves Saint Laurent.

Swiss Roll Pudding

¼ lb sifted sugar - 2 eggs the weight of one in flour.
Beat 2 yolks in a basin. add sugar - Beat whites
to a stiff froth - Mix altogether with a little baking
powder. Batter a tin & put the mixture in
evenly & bake for about 15 minutes -
Sprinkle castor sugar on the paste board turn
out - put jam on & roll at once

But it aint the time for sermons with the
we must try & help the girl that tommy's left behind
Cook's Son - Duke's Son - Son of a belted Earl
Son of a dambtle publican - its all the same to day "
Eacle of 'Em doing his Country's work & who'll look
after the girl. pass the hat for your Credits Sake & pay pay pay

Swiss Roll Pudding

4oz/110g sifted castor sugar
2oz/50g flour
2 eggs, separated
½ teaspoon baking powder
jam for spreading

Heat oven to 200°/gas mark 6. Line an 8"/20cm oblong Swiss Roll tray with greaseproof paper. Beat the egg yolks in a basin. Add the sugar, flour and baking powder. Whip egg whites to a stiff froth and fold into the mixture. Spread evenly on the tray and bake for 15 minutes. When cooked trim the edges, spread with jam and roll up at once.

It's called a pudding but I call it a cake. I was pleased when it turned out well because I thought it would be tricky to make but it was easier than I'd imagined.

Leche Crema

Beat up 3 eggs, leaving out two of the whites, & add to them gradually a pt & a ½ of milk, then mix carefully 4 table spoonsful of fine wheat flour, & two oz. of finely powdered loaf sugar, with grated lemon peel to give a flavour. Boil these ingredients over a slow fire, stirring constantly to prevent burning until the flour is quite dissolved. Prepare a shallow dish with some ratafia-cakes at the bottom & when the crema is sufficiently boiled pour it through a sieve upon the cakes — N.B. this delicious dish is always served up to the table cold. Just before sending up some powdered cinnamon should be dusted pretty thickly over it & This receipt was obtained from the Nuns of Santa Clara convent, at Palmas, in the island of Grand Canary

Leche Crema

3 egg yolks
1 egg white
1½ pints/845ml milk
4 tablespoons flour
2oz/50g castor sugar
grated rind of half a lemon
teaspoon powdered cinnamon
ratafia or amoretto biscuits

Prepare a shallow dish with the biscuits lining the bottom. Beat the egg yolks and the egg white. Gradually add the milk. Blend the flour, sugar and grated lemon carefully into the milk mixture. Bring to the boil very slowly to prevent burning. Stir constantly until the flour has dissolved. When sufficiently boiled and thickened pour mixture over the biscuits and leave to cool. Dust with the cinnamon before serving.

Leche is Spanish for milk. This is a lovely recipe. Creamy, smooth and soothing, and it keeps well in the fridge. It was eaten for two days running and the flavour of the almond biscuits intensified even more. Grandmother wrote that the recipe was obtained from the nuns of Santa Clara Convent in Las Palmas, Gran Canaria, one of the Canary Islands. The dessert is common throughout Latin America and Spain.

American Pudding

Requires no eggs.

2	Breakfast	cups of	Flour
1	"	" "	Chopped Suet
1	"	" "	Golden Syrup
1	teaspoonful		Cream of Tartar
1	"		Carbonate " Soda

a pinch of Salt & a few Sultanas or Currants
are an Improvement.

Mix well, tie in cloth leaving good room for
Swelling Put quickly in a saucepan of boiling
water not lifting the lid for an hour Boil 3
hours

American Pudding

2 cups flour
1 cup shredded suet
1½ cups golden treacle
1½ cups sultanas or currants
teaspoon cream of tartar
teaspoon bicarbonate of soda

Simply mix all the ingredients together and put into a lightly greased heatproof basin. Put a round of greaseproof paper over the top and cover the whole basin with a secure cloth or foil. Immerse in a large saucepan of simmering water making sure the water only comes halfway to the top of basin. Steam very slowly for 3 hours.

I said in the method 'simply mix' ingredients together - but the mixture was stiff. It was hard work so I ended up doing it by hand. It was not as sticky a job as one would imagine but even when completely mixed it still seemed heavy and doughy. I was almost too scared to cook it, thinking I was cooking a rock. But after 3 hours and as if by magic, out came a fabulous pudding.

Custard Pudding

Mix by degrees a pint of good milk
with a large spoonful of flour the
yolks of 5 eggs some orange flower water
& a little pounded cinnamon. Butter
a basin that will exactly hold it. Pour
the Batter & tie a floured Cloth over it.
put in boiling water over the fire &
turn it ~~&~~ about 5 Minutes to prevent
the egg going to one side
~~Half~~ an hour will boil it

Custard Pudding

1 pint/570ml milk
heaped tablespoon flour
5 egg yolks
teaspoon orange flower water or vanilla essence
tablespoon castor sugar
pinch of cinnamon

Butter a 2pt/1.2lt basin. Gradually blend the milk with the flour in a mixing bowl. Add the beaten egg yolks, orange water, or other flavouring, and the sugar. Pour this into the basin and cover with a cloth, foil or greaseproof paper. Put into a large saucepan of boiling water, making sure the water level only comes halfway to the top of basin and slowly simmer. For the first 5 minutes turn the basin occasionally to prevent mixture going to one side. Continue to boil gently for 30 minutes. When cooked sprinkle the top with the cinnamon.

Margaret Bond tested this recipe and added sugar. She was delighted with the results and now makes it often. The texture resembles double cream so it's perfect for pampering a fruit salad. Don't waste the egg whites but use them for the meringue recipe.

Apricot Creams

Pint of apricot   (after being passed through seives
     " " Cream
½ lb   Sugar
Table spoon full lemon essence & a few drops of
Chochineal
2 oz. of Gelatine

Take a tin of apricots & run them through lean
Sieve, Cream must be whipped & them mixed
with the apricots with Sugar & lemon juice added

Apricot Cream

14oz/411g tinned apricot halves in light syrup
2oz/50g castor sugar
5fl oz/150ml single cream
tablespoon lemon juice
1 sachet gelatine

Have ready a 1½pt/850ml dampened mould. Drain and purée the apricots. Stir in the sugar and cream. Heat, not boil, 5fl oz/150ml of the apricot syrup, sprinkle in the gelatine, stirring briskly till dissolved. Add immediately to the apricot mixture and when thoroughly blended pour into the dampened mould to set - about 4 hours.

The proof of the pudding is in the eating, and we did, until it was all gone. Delicate and delicious.

Strawberries Pudding

The weight of two eggs in flour & butter the weight of one in Sugar two tablespoonfuls of Strawberry Jam one teaspoonfull of carbonate of Soda, two eggs. Method Beat the eggs well & add them to the other ingredients except the Soda, which must be dissolved in a very little milk & added last of all. Put it in a buttered mould. It Should only half fill it & Steam for two hours & a half.

Strawberry Pudding

2 eggs
4oz/110g flour
4oz/110g melted butter
2oz/50g castor sugar
2 tablespoons strawberry jam
teaspoon bicarbonate of soda

Grease a basin large enough for the pudding to rise considerably. Beat the eggs well. Add all other ingredients except the soda which must be dissolved in a little milk and added last. Pour the mixture into the basin, cover with cloth or foil and steam for 2½ hours.

This was simple and resulted in a mouth-watering, light, steamed pudding. No wonder there are many steamed pudding recipes in the notebook. They are easy to prepare and always work. They are comfort eating, but the trouble is you always want more, and they are full of calories. But once in a while it can't hurt.

Banana Jelly

Six very ripe bananas a qr Lb of
Sugar the juice of half a lemon
one oz gelatine in a pint & a
half of cold water peel the Bananas
& mash them to a pulp add the Sugar
& lemon juice then mix this in with
the dissolved gelatine, Put it in to a
Saucepan & stir it over the fire
untill it boils pour into a wetted
mould, & let it stand untill quite
& set turn out & serve

Banana Jelly

6 ripe bananas
4oz/110g castor sugar
juice of half a lemon
2 sachets gelatine
6fl oz/150 ml water

Peel the bananas and mash to a pulp. Add the sugar and lemon juice. Heat, not boil, the water and sprinkle over the gelatine stirring briskly till dissolved. Add immediately to the banana mixture and blend together. Pour into a dampened mould or dish and leave to set in a cool place for about 4 hours.

Not being a fan of jelly I made half the quantity. That was a mistake because when I served it to my cousin and her two children they could not get enough of it and begged me to make it again. This seemed perfect for the cookery workshop at Ysgol y Castell. We made masses of it, and the children were delighted and felt proud that they had made the jelly themselves and it did not come from a packet.

Lemon Pudding

Half a lb of bread crumbs a qr of a lb ou
chopped Suet the rind of 2 lemons grated
& the juice of one two eggs well beaten;
mix the whole adde a qr lb of sugar sifted
& boil ¾ of an hour

Only some withered blossoms
Crumbling to dry decay
Only a glove half torn in two
And idly thrown away
Only a heart, that's breaking
That is if hearts, Can break
but a man adrift for life
all for a woman's sake
a few such tokens
do by a love sick fool
fht but the ashes that strew the fis
u loves

Lemon Pudding

8oz/225g breadcrumbs
4oz/110g chopped suet
6oz/175g castor sugar
juice and grated rind of 2 lemons
2 eggs

Grease a 1½pt/845ml basin. Mix the breadcrumbs, suet and sugar and add the lemon juice and grated rinds. Whisk the eggs and blend into the mixture. Put into a lightly greased heat resistant basin with a round of greaseproof paper on the top. Cover basin with a cloth or foil and place in a large saucepan of simmering water, making sure the water only comes halfway to the top of the basin. Steam for 1 hour.

Steamed puddings were popular with the Victorians. I cooked this for a luncheon party and was worried that it would be too heavy after the main course. Fortunately the whole pudding was eaten, and was especially enjoyed by the men.

Plum Pudding

1 lb Suet
1 " Currants
1 " Sultanas
1 " Raisins
1 " Flour
½ " Bread Crumbs
½ " Mixed peel
1 " Sugar
1 Nutmeg Spice to Taste

6 5 or 6 6 eggs
2 Lemons if liked

~~Stoped Stoe feu~~

or lb Stoes o lb Sugar fall 13 unsweetened jure
as them all work together 6 or 8 weeks
Shaking every day Shake & Bottle

Plum Pudding

4oz/110g shredded suet

4oz/110g currants

4oz/110g sultanas

4oz/110g raisins

4oz/110g castor sugar

4oz/110g flour

2oz/50g breadcrumbs

1 egg

teaspoon nutmeg

teaspoon baking powder

5fl oz/150ml milk

Grease a 2pt/1.2 litre basin. Mix all the dry ingredients with the suet. Add the egg. Gradually add the milk and mix to a dropping consistency. Put the mixture into the basin and cover the top with a circle of greaseproof paper. Cover the basin with foil or a cloth. Put a tin plate at the bottom of a large saucepan, place the basin on this and steam for 5 hours or more. After 5 hours insert a knife and if it comes out clean then it's done.

The original quantities for this pudding were vast so I reduced them and I still had a pudding for at least 8 people. I couldn't believe how simple this was to make. One just has to be a bit patient with the cooking time.

The Husbands Commandments

I I am thy husband whom thou didst vow to, love, honour and obey, for I saved the from old maidism and the terrors of single blessedness

II Thou shalt not look upon any other man to love or admire him; for I thy husband am a jealous man, who will visit the sins of the wife upon her followers. therefore keep thou faithfully to the marriage vows.

III Thou shalt not back bite thy husband or speak lightly of him, neither shalt thou expose his faults to thy neighbour lest he should hear of it and punish thy perfidy by a privation of sundry items, such as bonnets, dresses, and etc.

IIII Thou shalt purchase cigars for thy husband rather than ribbons for thyself

IIIII Thou shalt not go to the opera or evening parties, without thy husband, neither shalt thou dance too frequently with thy cousin or thy husbands friend

6 Thou shalt not ~~rifle thy husbands~~ listen to flattery nor accept gifts or trinkets from any man save thy husband

7 Thou shalt not rifle thy husbands pockets
for money, when he is asleep neither shalt
thou read any letters thou mayst find therein
for it is his business to look after his own affairs
and thine to let his alone

8 Thou shalt conceal nothing from thy husband

9 Thou shalt make no false representations of
the state of thy pantry thy purse or thy wardrobe

10 Remember to rise early in the morning & so
prepare with becoming good humour to welcome thy
husband at the breakfast table

11 Look for no jewellery, from thy husband
on the Anniversary of thy wedding day
for it is written blessed are they who expect
nothing, for they shall not be disappointed

B. Leonard

Acknowledgements

~

My thanks to my testers and tasters:

The American Women's Association, Morocco; Mary Arthur - Williams; Kay Cluseau; Margaret Bond; Raymond Bowers and Michael Lancod; Sue Batt; Bobby Crush; Richard Fox; Geoffrey Hutchings; Pam Jones; Alan Kreppel; David Kenna; Valerie Leveton; Diana Lidstone; Christine Maskell; The Mermaids of the Three Rivers Hotel & Spa, Ferryside; Pembrokeshire Historic Buildings Trust; The Pearl Brasserie, Dublin; Kirsten Batt and Sebastien Masi; John Rubin; Tricia Stone; Stradey Park Hotel, Llanelli; Stephen Jones; Gavin Alexander; Ysgol y Castell, Kidwelly; Victor Spinetti; John Bates and John Siggins.

And thanks, also, to:

Peggy and Mollie Thomas; Brian and Janet Coleman; Shirley and Ian Norman, The Boat House Gallery, Little Haven; Andi Sloss; Barry Saunders; Owen J Vaughan; Jane Wareham; Carmarthen County Museum.

Index

∾

Index

❧